Mason Long

The life of Mason Long, the Converted Gambler

Mason Long

The life of Mason Long, the Converted Gambler

ISBN/EAN: 9783744715836

Printed in Europe, USA, Canada, Australia, Japan

Cover: Foto ©Lupo / pixelio.de

More available books at **www.hansebooks.com**

MASON LONG,
THE
CONVERTED GAMBLER.

THE LIFE

OF

MASON LONG,

THE

Converted Gambler.

BEING A RECORD OF HIS EXPERIENCE AS A WHITE SLAVE; A SOLDIER IN THE UNION ARMY; A PROFESSIONAL GAMBLER; A PATRON OF THE TURF; A VARIETY THEATER AND MINSTREL MANAGER; AND, FINALLY, A CONVERT TO THE MURPHY CAUSE, AND TO THE GOSPEL OF CHRIST.

WRITTEN BY HIMSELF.

WITH A PORTRAIT, AND SIX ILLUSTRATIONS.

CHICAGO:
DONNELLEY, LOYD & CO., PRINTERS.
1878.

ENTERED ACCORDING TO ACT OF CONGRESS, IN THE YEAR 1878, BY

I. S. FELGER,

IN THE OFFICE OF THE LIBRARIAN OF CONGRESS AT WASHINGTON.

TO
JOHN D. OLDS, Esq.,
OF

FORT WAYNE, IND.,

THIS LITTLE BOOK IS AFFECTIONATELY DEDICATED, IN TOKEN OF GRATI-
TUDE FOR THE GREAT KINDNESS
RECEIVED FROM HIM, AND FOR THE RESPECT ENTERTAINED
FOR HIS HIGH CHRISTIAN CHARACTER, AND HIS
UNSELFISH BENEVOLENCE, BY

THE AUTHOR.

TABLE OF CONTENTS.

	PAGE
PREFACE,	15

CHAPTER I.

My boyhood and youth—Seven years of abject slavery—Hard lessons of the ways of the world—I become a Union soldier, ... 17

CHAPTER II.

My career as a soldier—The routine of camp life—Bloody battles, forced marches, and long sieges—Record of three eventful years, ... 23

CHAPTER III.

My first experience in gambling—Prevalence of the vice among officers and soldiers—Heavy winnings during the war—Playing under difficulties—My first taste of liquor—The Fort Wayne confidence gang, . . 37

CHAPTER IV.

How I degenerated from a business man into a professional gambler—Severe lessons at my new trade—My sad experience as manager of a minstrel troupe and proprietor of a variety theater at Lafayette—Ups and downs as a gambler—A faro game stopped by a fearful powder explosion, ... 57

CHAPTER V.

The horrors of delirium tremens—Visions of the "White Mice"—Repeated captures by the police—Ludicrous flight of a bloodthirsty sport—Large winnings invested in a palatial saloon and gambling den—Reckless dissipation and prodigality—An hour in jail—Low ebb of fortune, ... 76

CHAPTER VI.

" Following the trotters "—Sights and scenes on the turf —Make-shifts of a broken gambler—"Canada Bill's" confidence operations — Traveling on "cheek"— A fourteen weeks debauch—Another horrible experience with delirium tremens, ... 96

CHAPTER VII.

The various phases of gambling—Good and bad qualities of the genuine sporting man — Prevalence of the vice among business men — The misery and ruin it causes—A few words to the sporting fraternity, . . 125

CHAPTER VIII.

How I became a convert to the Murphy cause— Signing the pledge—Struggles with the demon alcohol— Final triumph over the rum devil, ... 144

CHAPTER IX.

My conversion to the Gospel of Jesus Christ—Mental sufferings while under conviction—Public confession of my sins—The blessings attending a change of heart, ... 160

CHAPTER X.

My admission into the First Baptist Church of Fort Wayne—Immersion in the presence of a vast audience—Press reports of the ceremony, . . . 182

CHAPTER XI.

My career since my conversion—What I am doing in the temperance work, ... 200

CHAPTER XII.

Supplementary chapter, written by my pastor, Dr. J. R. Stone, at my request, ... 211

CHAPTER XIII.

Extract from "The Ribbon Workers," edited by J. M. Hiatt, Esq., and published by J. W. Goodspeed, Chicago, ... 225

PREFACE.

I HAVE no apology to offer for writing this little book. I have not the assurance to claim for it any especial literary merit, or any permanent value. But my life, though short, has been a rather eventful one, and I have told it truthfully in the hope that my readers — and especially the young — will take warning from my follies and crimes, and realize from my experience that "The way of the Transgressor is hard." As I look back with sorrow and remorse upon the worse than wasted years of my manhood, I pray that others may be spared my suffering. If in my youth there had been placed before me the sad tale of some unfortunate human being, whose life had been wrecked by dissipation and debauchery, I believe my career would have been very different. I earnestly hope that this unpretending little volume may be the means of saving some young man from my bitter experience, and causing him to realize the beauty and happiness of an upright, sober, and virtuous life.

I ask the reader's indulgence as to the literary defects of my book, of which no one can be more conscious than myself.

MASON LONG.

MASON LONG,

THE

CONVERTED GAMBLER.

MASON LONG.

CHAPTER I.

MY BOYHOOD AND YOUTH—SEVEN YEARS OF ABJECT SLAVERY—HARD LESSONS OF THE WAYS OF THE WORLD —I BECOME A UNION SOLDIER.

The story of my life is not a pleasant one. It will not excite the admiration or enthusiasm of the reader. It is not characterized — would to God it were — by great deeds, noble actions, high impulses. My career has been in no way different from that of thousands of others, excepting that, through the grace of God, it was altered before I had drank the bitter cup to the very dregs. My story is that of a bleak and cheerless childhood, a youth of ignorance and hardship, a manhood of intemperance and vice.

I was born in Luray, Licking County, Ohio, on the 10th of September, 1842. My father, Jacob Long, died at the age of fifty-six, when I was but six years old. After his death I went with my mother, Margaret Long, a noble Christian woman, to West Salem, Ashland County, Ohio, where my grandfather lived.

I remained there until my mother died, leaving me all alone in the world. Although but ten years of age, the scene at her death-bed made an impression upon my memory which time can never efface. After years of sinful indulgence, during which her dying words, though often called to mind, had failed to awaken my seared and deadened conscience, they came back to me with a new and vivid meaning, and I at last thanked God that the prayer which my dear mother uttered with her parting breath had been answered.

Left at this tender age an orphan, homeless, friendless, and penniless, my boyhood was, indeed, a bleak and cheerless one. I was bound out to a wealthy German farmer, of Medina County, Ohio, whose abject slave I was for seven years. They were years of hard labor, and cruel treatment; years which brought to me only sadness and suffering; years of gloom and servitude, unrelieved by one kind word, or one tender glance. But although deprived of home, friends, family, of all those surroundings which make childhood the pleasantest portion of many lives, I never ceased to look forward to a better day ahead. Well has the poet said:

> Hope springs eternal in the human breast,
> Man never is, but always to be blest.

It made no difference how severe my task,

how cruel my treatment, how dreary my life, I never ceased to hope for a happier future.

The terms of my apprenticeship were that I was to labor for my employer until I reached the age of eighteen, receiving my board and clothes, with two months of schooling each year; I was also to have a horse and saddle.

Mr. K., my employer — I may say owner — put me at work immediately in clearing land, and for five years I was never away from the clearings for a single day. That whole section was a forest when I entered it, and the labor of felling the trees and clearing the land was very severe. A part of the time I worked in a large sugar camp, where we made eighteen hundred pounds of sugar, and six hundred gallons of maple syrup, every spring. I remained in this slavery — for it was nothing else — for seven years, during which time we cleared one hundred acres of land, and my master erected a large residence and fine barn, besides paying for his real estate. His treatment of me was very inhuman. No slave-holder of the South ever treated his black chattels as barbarously as this brute in human form treated me, and to his harshness and inhumanity I ascribe much of my subsequent sinful career. I was deprived of all the usual happy accompaniments of childhood. In seven years I only went to school three months. I was scarcely allowed sufficient clothing to hide my nakedness, and was not permitted to associate with other children; when my relatives came to see me, I was denied the privilege of speaking to them. Once I stole out and talked to them a few moments, and for this I was brutally beaten with a large black-snake whip, carrying the marks of the punishment upon my back for several months. When I reached the age of seventeen, I determined to be a slave no longer, and although I had one year more to serve, my guardian secured my freedom. I left my brutal taskmaster in a pitiable condition. My entire wardrobe consisted of a piece of a straw hat, a pair of blue overalls, and two "hickory" shirts. I had no coat and no shoes; I was in total ignorance of the world, could scarcely read, had never been inside of a church but three or four times, and did not know what a Sabbath school was. As I left the scene of my youthful hardships, wondering what the future had in store for me, I looked back over the preceding seven years to the day of my mother's death. She died at the house of my unfeeling master, and when her body was taken to the grave, I, a boy of ten, was compelled to stand some distance away and hold the horses, being denied the poor privilege of seeing the coffin lowered into the ground. Well do I remember with what utter sorrow and despair

I left the cemetery, and what sad anticipations filled my little heart, anticipations which proved only too well founded.

I can not think kindly of the man who thus reared me in ignorance and prepared me for a life of wickedness and shame. His avarice and cruelty have made him rich in this world's goods. I would not injure him if I could, but leave him with the Divine Ruler, who shall at last judge us all. After gaining my freedom, I worked for a neighboring farmer for a short time, and obtained some clothes and a little money. At Wellington, Ohio, I purchased a ticket for Rock Island, Ill., and then for the first time I saw a railroad. I obtained work on a farm near Geneseo, Ill., at sixteen dollars a month. The next winter I worked for my board and went to school, and then for the first time did I realize my pitiable ignorance.

In a short time I had another severe experience of the ways of the world. I obtained work for which I was to receive seventeen dollars a month, and being anxious to save money I only drew five dollars during ten months, at the expiration of which time my employer sold out and decamped, leaving me unpaid. I followed him to Chicago, but he refused to pay me, and only laughed at my entreaties. I returned to Geneseo a disheartened boy. I then went to school for a short time, and again obtained work on a farm. While engaged in this occupation, I was unfortunate enough to be arrested on a charge of stealing a set of harness. Of this offense I am glad to say that I was entirely innocent; indeed, the man who caused my arrest admitted, when I was brought up for examination, that he knew nothing about the case, and I was discharged without a hearing. This was the first, but alas! not the last time, that I was arrested, and the event made an ineffaceable impression upon my mind.

After this I went to work for myself. I first purchased a yoke of oxen and worked them for a while, then traded them for a horse, and engaged in buying and selling cattle. I was doing well at this, but in the Spring of 1862, when good Uncle Abraham was calling for more troops to defend the Union against the assault of its foes, I felt it was my duty to respond, and I enrolled my name in the 112th Illinois Volunteers.

The reader may think I have gone too much into detail in relating the history of my childhood and youth; but I desired to show the influences with which I was surrounded, and the atmosphere in which I grew to manhood, and which explain to a great extent the folly and wickedness of my after life.

CHAPTER II.

MY CAREER AS A SOLDIER—THE ROUTINE OF CAMP LIFE —BLOODY BATTLES, FORCED MARCHES, AND LONG SIEGES—RECORD OF THREE EVENTFUL YEARS.

In the Spring of 1862, I, in company with a number of my companions, enrolled my name in the 112th Regiment, Illinois Volunteer Infantry, as a private, and served in that capacity until the war closed. Our regiment went into camp at Peoria, and remained there about four weeks, when we were transferred to Covington, Ky. We were in camp near that place for some time, when we were removed to Lexington, Ky. There we remained in camp till the Spring of 1863. General Granger commanded our division. Until that time our life had been very monotonous, nothing but drilling and camp duty having been required of us. We were very restive, and longed for active service, of which we soon got enough to satisfy the most sanguinary among us.

Our first fighting was with John Morgan, the notorious guerilla, whom we pursued all over central Kentucky, and with whom we had a number of skirmishes. In the Fall of 1863, we crossed the Cumberland Mountains into

East Tennessee, our army being then under command of General A. E. Burnside, a most brave and accomplished officer, at present a United States Senator from the State of Rhode Island, of which he was recently the governor. Our march over the mountains was a severe one, abounding in hardships and privations which were very rigorous, after the prolonged indolence of camp life. A great many of our horses and mules died on the road, and the stench from their carcasses was almost unendurable. We were on short rations, and suffered greatly from lack of water. Immediately after reaching Tennessee, fighting commenced in good earnest. From that time until we were mustered out of service, we had scarcely any rest. Our first general engagement in Tennessee was that of Philadelphia (then Campbell Station), and was a bloody and closely contested one. We were defeated with considerable loss, and were driven by the enemy to Knoxville. They at once laid siege to the city, and maintained it for eighteen days. On the 18th of November, our brigade was stationed two miles from the city, for the purpose of holding the enemy in check until the citizens and negroes could throw up entrenchments for the protection of the town. This was a terrible day, and one which I can never forget. The battle began at daybreak, and the bloody work continued until nightfall. We were stationed on the brow of a hill, and had no breastworks, our only protection being a rail fence, of which we made good use. We piled the rails closely together, and they were of much service to us. The force of the minnie balls which struck the rails was almost spent when they reached us. But nevertheless, the mortality among our soldiers was very great; many of our brave boys were killed and wounded that day, gladly giving up their life's blood for their country, and nerving their companions, by their heroism, to renewed exertions. Blessed be the memory of the thousands whose bones are bleaching on Southern battle-fields, and whose deeds of bravery and valor call forth the enthusiasm of the historian, and the glowing eloquence of the poet.

The firing between the two armies was maintained during the entire day. We frequently ran out of ammunition, when it became necessary to go to the rear, half a mile distant, after a new supply. This was a trying ordeal, and taxed the nerve of our boys to the utmost. It required not a little bravery to start back with the ammunition, and face a scorching fire for half a mile. Many were killed and wounded in making the attempt, and it seemed almost miraculous that any passed unharmed through the shower of bullets that fell so thickly around them.

About four o'clock in the afternoon, the enemy brought the contest to a crisis by making a grand charge upon us. The colonel of the Sixth Georgia regiment rode up to the rail fence, I have mentioned, and called upon us to surrender. Our colonel gave the command to fire, and the poor fellow never asked any one to surrender again. About one-half of our company shot at him, and his body was literally riddled with bullets. The engagement then waxed hotter, and when the cannon balls struck the fence, the rails flew like so many feathers.

About this time, the brave Gen. Saunders, who commanded our division, was killed. One of our boys, who was wounded, was hobbling to to the rear, when Gen. Saunders took his gun from him, and, as he was about firing, a ball struck him, and he never spoke again.

At this stage of the battle, a most desperate conflict was in progress. The rebels had climbed over the fence, and were fighting hand to hand with our troops. The "Johnnies" were so intermingled with our men, that it was almost impossible to tell them apart. Our boys were greatly demoralized by Saunders' loss, and we did not stand our ground much longer. We hurriedly retreated, falling back two miles, through open fields, under a raking cross-fire from the rebel artillery. Our losses were frightful. Many of our comrades yielded their lives upon this retreat, and many more were deprived of arms and legs, and made physical wrecks for life. It was with great difficulty that we secured the bodies of our officers who had been killed, but as true soldiers we would not leave them on the field. The captain of Co. A, of our regiment, had been shot all to pieces by a shell. We saved his body, and that of Gen. Saunders, and carried them two miles under a sweeping fire, when we made a halt. At the dead hour of night, the American flag was wrapped around them, and both were buried in one grave. The interment was made amidst profound silence, not even the roll of a muffled drum being allowed, lest it should apprise the enemy of our loss. These men died true heroes, and their memories will always be revered by those who shared their perils. The fort at Knoxville was named for Gen. Saunders, in honor of his bravery. Our dead and wounded fell into the hands of the enemy. We retired into Knoxville, and the Confederates laid siege to us; we were penned up in the city for eighteen days, and were exposed to many perils and hardships; our situation was very critical, and we did not know at what hour we might have to surrender. Our losses were quite heavy, many of our sentinels being shot by the rebel sharpshooters, who were very skillful, killing men with neatness and dispatch at a distance of three-quarters of a mile. One day we ventured to make a charge upon a beautiful residence about a mile from our entrenchments, burning the building, and driving the enemy back. This was done for the purpose of saving the lives of our outer guard. During the siege, our horses suffered greatly; we had no grain, and, in order to afford them sustenance, we felled large trees, and they browsed off the branches. They literally stripped the trees, even eating the bark. During the last week of the siege, we took the poorest horses across the river, and shot them, fifty at a time; in one field were the dead bodies of more than fifteen hundred horses and mules.

Never had a morning looked so lovely to us as that of the day upon which this memorable siege was raised. As day dawned we saw the Union troops approaching in the distance, and knew that we were saved at last. As the reinforcements approached, our brave boys gave way to their feelings, and rent the air with loud shouts and hearty huzzas. The enemy hastily "pulled up stakes," and started in the direction of Bean Station, where they made a halt; at that point a hard fight took place, and we lost part of our wagon train. The Confederates continued their retreat from Bean

Station to Muddy Creek, where there was bloody fighting in the woods. At the latter place our Col. Brownlow, a son of " Parson " Brownlow, was captured. The rebels did not know who he was. He purchased his freedom for twenty dollars, and was soon with us again. We pursued the enemy to Dandridge, and then to Kelley's Ford, where there was sharp fighting for a time. Shortly after this, our troops were transferred to Middle Tennessee, and thence to Georgia. In the latter State, we saw some hard service, the severest contest being in front of Atlanta, on the 6th of August, where many of the brave members of the 112th surrendered their lives. Atlanta fell, and the Union army continued its victorious march southward, fighting every day. It was in one of the engagements about Atlanta, that the noble Gen. McPherson was killed.

There was hot work before us. Sherman soon started on his memorable march to the sea, and our regiment became a part of the army commanded by that brave officer, General Geo. H. Thomas. We left at once for Tennessee, and soon came in contact with the Confederate army commanded by General Hood. Here we entered upon the hardest campaign of marching and fighting that we experienced during our service. Hood's army pressed us closely, and we were on the retreat for many days, fighting at every step. When we reached Franklin, Tennessee, only five hours in advance of our pursuers, we made a stand and hastily prepared for battle; we improved our time by throwing up breastworks. As we worked we could see the enemy approaching for a long distance, and we knew there was going to be a severe conflict. And so it proved. We were stationed in the center on the Pike Road. The rebels dashed upon us in nine lines of battle, and we received them with a raking cross fire from our artillery; we poured volley after volley into their ranks, but it did not even check their advance. These brave soldiers kept steadily advancing, pressing forward to our works, although at every step many fell wounded and dying under our sweeping fire. Like the Light Brigade they literally pushed

"Into the jaws of death,
Into the mouth of hell."

Here the Confederate General Pat. Claiborne performed a deed of bravery and gallantry which is unsurpassed in the annals of the war, and paid his life as a forfeit. In order to gain a foothold for his men, General Claiborne planted spurs in his gray charger, and dashed to the top of our earthworks. He gained the pinnacle before a shot touched him, but just as he reached the highest point, horse and rider went down together in the presence of both armies. It seemed as though a thousand shots were fired at him. The sight was a memorable one, and, enemy though he was, we could not but honor him for his wonderful daring. The deed was a fitting one for the poet and painter to immortalize.

Through General Claiborne's heroism the enemy succeeded in breaking our lines. An Ohio regiment gave way, and three thousand Confederates poured in upon us. This was the crisis of the battle, and for a time it seemed as if the annihilation of General Thomas' entire army was inevitable; but the gallant Twenty-fourth Kentucky made a bold charge, closing up the gap and saving the Union army. The heavy firing then ceased, and there was a lull in the roar of battle. The two armies were so close to each other, that the "Yankees" and the "Johnnies" could easily converse together, only our earthworks separating the foes. The air was laden with the groans of the wounded and the shrieks of the dying, and the blue and the gray mingled their prayers together as they passed into the hereafter. Many of the poor fellows cried piteously for water, but fate denied them even that little boon, and with parched lips and burning tongues they lingered until death ended their sufferings. We remained in this position for three hours, for the purpose of holding the enemy in check while our wagon train was crossing the river; we then began our retreat, leaving our wounded in the enemy's hands. The poor fellows pleaded and begged to be taken with us, but it was impossible, as we could with difficulty save ourselves. Many of the boys wept as they started off, leaving their wounded comrades on the field of battle. Thus ended one of the most sanguinary battles of the war, considering the number of men engaged and the time occupied. We quietly crossed the river and retreated towards Nashville. The march was a hard one — much of it being made in double-quick time. We reached Nashville but a little in advance of the enemy.

On the first day after our arrival we were stationed at Fort Negley, but were then ordered off to the right, where we saw more bloody work. During the second day's fight we charged the enemy and were repulsed with heavy loss, leaving our wounded again on the field. The night was a very severe one, and many of our wounded boys perished from the cold.

Among those killed that day was my brother. On this day we succeeded in recapturing our dead and wounded. They presented a horrible spectacle, and one never to be forgotten; among them were several hundred colored troops. At last we had obtained a decided advantage over

Gen. Hood's troops, and forced them to retreat. We pressed them so hard that they drowned artillery in every stream they passed, until they were almost disarmed. We pursued Hood to the river at Clifton, Tennessee, and captured a large portion of his command.

The scenes were then shifted and we were transferred to another sphere of action. From Clifton we were taken by the fleet to Cincinnati, and thence by rail to Washington. We were then hurried to Alexandria, and after a brief delay embarked on board the steamer Atlantic for Fort Fisher. The Atlantic was an old hulk which had been used many years for mail service between New York and Liverpool, and had been pronounced unseaworthy. The underwriters had refused to insure her, but the government thought she was good enough for soldiers. Supposing she was lost, with all on board, it would only be a few soldiers, that was all; none of the government officials at Washington could risk any thing.

The trip was a memorable one. The Atlantic carried three thousand five hundred infantry and the Ohio Battery of artillery, with Major General J. D. Cox, now member of Congress from the Toledo district, in command. We stopped at Fortress Monroe, and took one million rounds of ammunition. We made no other stops until we reached our destination.

We "land lubbers" found this voyage any thing but a pleasant one. In going around Cape Hatteras we experienced those peculiar sensations which only those can appreciate who have "been there;" our regiment was in the "hold," about ten feet below water, and we did not succumb as soon as those on the hurricane deck. The boys of the 140th Indiana were up there, and they began to "feed the sea gulls" three hours ahead of us. When I was attacked I thought my time had come, for the sensations I experienced were deathly. When the Atlantic climbed the waves of Hatteras every joint in her cracked, and we constantly expected her to go to pieces. We remained in sight of Fort Fisher— sometimes called Federal Point—three days before we landed We went to shore in little tug boats, and had at first but two miles of a foothold. We marched up the Cape Fear River, took Fort Anderson, and then proceeded to Wilmington, N. C.; our path lay through the dense pineries, first to Goldsboro and then to Raleigh; at this place we first heard of the assassination of President Lincoln. The news created the utmost indignation and excitement among our troops, and they determined to burn the beautiful city for revenge. Our commander gave strict orders against any such proceedings, and detached three thousand trusty

veterans as a protection against incendiarism.
From Raleigh we went to Greensboro, and there
we heard the glad news that Lee had surrendered; Johnson had already succumbed, and
now we knew that the civil war was over,
and that the cause for which we had fought
and struggled so long was victorious. We
unfurled the American flag from the tops of
the highest trees, and exhibited our joy and
happiness in many ways. We remained in
camp at Greensboro some time, and were then
mustered out of the service. We proceeded
home *via* Baltimore, and reaching Chicago on
the Fourth of July, where we were paid off,.
we indulged in a general jollification, and many
of us gave way to riotous excesses. We had
ended our career as soldiers, and were civilians
once again.

Brigadier General T. J. Henderson, of Princeton, Ill., was our commander during the entire
war. He now represents the Sixth Illinois
District in Congress. He was a brave officer,
and enjoyed the respect and affection of his
men in a remarkable degree. While we were
serving under him in Kentucky he was nominated to fill the unexpired term of Lovejoy in
Congress. He was a strict disciplinarian, and
as we were unused to the rigor of military life,
we deemed him arbitrary and tyrannical, and
many of us wrote letters to his district urging

his defeat on those grounds. These letters I have no doubt worked his defeat upon that occasion, and are deeply regretted by many of the writers, who afterward learned to love the general for his bravery and kindheartedness. When the regiment was mustered out of service there was not a boy in it who would not have fought for General Henderson. He did his duty bravely from the beginning to the end of the war, and well merited his promotion from private to brigadier general.

Our old regiment has held annual reunions since the war, four of which I have attended. It is very pleasant for the men who shared so many perils together to assemble and recount the experience of their three eventful years of army life. We have resolved to hold a reunion every year so long as two of us survive. General Henderson — God bless him — is with us heart and soul.

CHAPTER III.

MY FIRST EXPERIENCE IN GAMBLING—PREVALENCE OF THE VICE AMONG OFFICERS AND SOLDIERS—HEAVY WINNINGS DURING THE WAR—PLAYING UNDER DIFFICULTIES—MY FIRST TASTE OF LIQUOR—THE FORT WAYNE CONFIDENCE GANG.

When I enlisted in the United States Army, in 1862, I had never tasted liquor, nor touched a card. During the service I formed many bad habits, among them that of gambling. I first began playing with members of my mess, when we were stationed at Lexington, Ky., and proved an apt scholar. I was soon able to win money from men who had gambled for years, and who, one would think, would know all about it. I formed the acquaintance of Johnny White, an expert sport belonging to the 100th Ohio regiment, and he taught me, for twenty-five dollars, a trick of working cards, by means of which I won large sums of money. In this way I realized four hundred dollars after the first pay-day subsequent to learning the trick. I had never had so much money before, at one time, and I did not know how to use it. I spent it very freely, soon finding myself out of funds. I then contracted habits of recklessness and extravagance which adhered to me during my entire life as a "man of the world." I rapidly became a spendthrift and squandered money freely with the sutlers and any one who had any thing to sell. I indulged largely in luxuries, regardless of expense.

I rapidly mastered the mysteries of poker, casino, chuck-a-luck, and other games, and soon acquired a considerable notoriety as a gambler. Playing became a perfect mania among the soldiers, and many gambled—including church members and professing Christians—who had never thought of doing so before. Gaming afforded relief to the monotony of camp-life and produced excitement which withdrew the attention of the boys from the perils they were undergoing. Notwithstanding my speedily acquired notoriety as a gambler, I stood well with my officers, and for a long time they overlooked my propensities in this direction. I continued playing the trick I had learned, very successfully, and wandered off into different regiments for the purpose of reaping a harvest, through its operation. Upon one occasion I was absent upon an expedition of this kind for ten successive roll-calls, and was reported as a deserter. During my absence I had been playing some heavy games of poker. I finally returned to my regiment with thirteen hundred and fifty dollars winnings in my pocket. I was at once arraigned as a deserter before a regimental court martial, over which Lieutenant-Colonel Bond presided. He had always seemed partial to me, and I had little fear of the result when the trial opened. I had a physician's certificate of unfitness for duty in my pocket, but I felt so confident of the result that I did not show it, fearing that if I did, I would compromise the surgeon who gave it. I was soon adjudged guilty. Colonel Bond, upon whom fell the duty of administering the sentence, said, with a look and tone of sternness, that my transgressions had been repeated and flagrant, and that he proposed to make an example of me. I trembled at these words, fearing that I was doomed to six months' hard labor upon the fortifications, with a ball and chain, which was the extreme penalty. The colonel proceeded, however, to sentence me to forfeit a month's pay, amounting to thirteen dollars, and to three days' extra work in digging sinks. I was overjoyed at the lightness of the penalty. The thirteen dollars, of course, I did not miss out of my large roll, and the three days' labor I cheerfully performed. I feared that this proceeding would render it impossible for me to get an honorable discharge, at the close of the war, but such was not the case.

So strong was the fascination which the vice of gambling cast over the men, that they risked their lives to indulge their passion for it. Many games of chuck-a-luck and poker were played on the skirmish line while the bullets were flying thick and fast about us, and occasionally taking some poor fellow to his long home.

At night, the men congregated in the woods, whenever possible, and played by the flickering light of torches. I remember one night, while we were in Georgia, that about one hundred and fifty men were in a thickly-timbered piece of woods, near Snake Creek Gap, engaged in this pursuit, when a detachment raided them, under orders from the brigade headquarters. I had been sitting on a log, conducting a game of chuck-a-luck, with a torch bearer by my side, whom I paid ten dollars per night for his services. I was sitting on my winnings, which amounted to four hundred and fifty dollars, when we were surrounded; the torch holder at once blew out the light, and, as I rolled off the log to secrete myself, he seized the money. I escaped arrest, but a large number of men were marched up to headquarters.

"What is the charge against these men?" asked the officer.

"Gambling," was the reply.

"Is Mace Long among them?" was the next question.

"No, sir, we did n't see him."

"Well, then, let the others go. It is not right to punish any body, when the chief offender goes free."

This illustrates the estimation in which I had come to be held. Many of the officers themselves liked to gamble as well as the private soldiers did. I played many times with officers, and found numerous expert gamesters among them. Immediately after the battle of Franklin, we retreated to Nashville. In company with White, whom I have before referred to, I rode into Nashville on a freight train. Being without passports, we were taken by the guards to the Zollicoffer House, which had been converted, temporarily, into a prison, and which was filled with both Federals and Confederates. The building was crowded, and many of the inmates were filthy and swarming with vermin. The place was a decidedly uncomfortable one, and we longed to regain our freedom as soon as possible. White was looking through a window upon the street, when he happened to see an Ohio colonel, with whom he was well acquainted. To him we related the circumstances, and through his exertions we were released from our terrible confinement. In his company, we proceeded to a hotel, and, after supper, were introduced to a railroad conductor, when a game of poker was agreed upon. I had left a deck of marked cards at the office of the hotel, and by previous arrangement, when cards were called for, these were brought to the room. White and I played against the colonel and the conductor, and when we rose from the table at two o'clock in the morning, we had relieved them of one thousand dollars. The reader will probably regard this as a poor return for the officer's kindness to us, and so it was. The next morning I joined my regiment at Fort Negley. Despite my recklessness, I never shirked duty to indulge in gambling, and I at least have the satisfaction of knowing that I was always on hand, whenever there was any fighting to be done. I never missed a skirmish or general engagement in which my regiment participated, during the entire war, excepting when I was in the hospital, where I spent two months.

I usually won when I played with the officers, but not always so. Once I received a written invitation to visit the general's headquarters. I went there, not knowing what I was wanted for, and upon arriving found two *aides-de-camp* engaged in a game of poker, which they requested me to join. Of course, I complied; I lost six or seven hundred dollars; I dropped one hundred dollars on my last hand, and, finally getting out of funds, stopped as I commenced — by request. My invitation to participate in the game was due to the knowledge that I had a little money, but after that experience, I viewed games where such formalities were used with great suspicion.

Most of my large winnings were made on chuck-a-luck. This may be briefly described as a game, where the more you lay down, the less you pick up. The percentage in favor of the game against the outsider, is at least fifty per cent., and the latter is sure to lose if he plays any length of time. The game is a simple one. Upon a piece of oil-cloth are marked various squares, numbered from one to six, inclusive, thus:

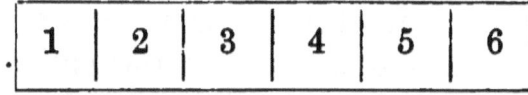

The player places his money upon one of these figures and the dealer throws three dice. If the dice turn up the number bet on, the game loses the amount wagered. If the number is up twice, the player receives double the sum he has risked, etc. It will readily be seen that the manager of the game has an absolute certainty to win, unless he falls into the hands of old sports who are too smart for him. I will give an illustration: Once a new recruit came among us and attempted to conduct a game. He had entered as a substitute, and the money thus obtained, together with the proceeds of his game, amounted to fourteen hundred dollars. I played against him, and in thirty minutes had won all he had, and he owed me seventy five dollars. This is not contradictory of my assertion as to the relative chances of dealer and player, as the reader will soon perceive. I won by working in a "ringer" upon him. By a "ringer" I mean a dice which I carried, and which I had altered so that it had five five-spots and one six spot. I had cut in holes with my knife, blackened them with a pencil, and while making change had abstracted one of his dice and substituted my "ringer" for it. Of course I had a sure thing to win, as I bet my money on the five-spot. In order to get my "ringer" back I took the dealer's "kit"—worth perhaps five dollars, for the seventy-five dollars which he owed me.

Chuck-a-luck was the popular game after pay-day. Then I would spread my cloths and reap a rich harvest. Frequently the men had no facilities for sending their money home, and this led them to risk it in play. I once won seven hundred dollars on this game while waiting for dinner to be cooked at a farm house, and this was by no means a remarkable case. Although I knew I was sure to lose, the gambling spell was so strong upon me, that I sometimes played against this game, and once lost fifteen hundred dollars in this manner in less than half an hour.

When the first few days after pay-day had passed, and the amateur sports found themselves broke, our playing was confined to the "bankers" and the officers, and upon these games very large sums changed hands.

The reader must not imagine from what has been related, that every soldier was addicted to the vice of gambling. Although a great many yielded to its influence, there were numerous good men who resisted it. We had in our company a noble, religious man named Lauferty, from Cambridge, Ill., who frequently cautioned me against this sin, and predicted the consequences if I continued to indulge in it. I paid no heed to his words, and thought him over scrupulous; nevertheless I had great confidence in him. In North Carolina, in the Spring of 1865, the men had just received six months' pay. This fact, together with the general anticipation of a big battle and the impossibility of remitting money to the North, gave an unprecedented stimulus to gambling. It is a singular fact that the men always played more recklessly upon the eve of a great battle than at any other time. I won heavily about this time, and had forty-three hundred dollars in cash. I offered Mr. Lauferty eighteen hundred dollars of it to keep for me, so that if I should be captured by the enemy I would not lose all I had. Imagine my surprise when he refused to touch it, because it was made by gambling. I thought him very silly then, but I hold a different opinion now.

During the war my net winnings amounted to eleven thousand dollars, part of which I spent, and the remainder I sent to my relatives at Geneseo, Ill.

After leaving the army in 1865, I proceeded to Geneseo, and thence to Fort Wayne where, in August, I opened a grocery and provision store, in which I invested two thousand eight hundred dollars of my gambling spoils. I started out with fair prospects and a determination to succeed. I introduced a novelty in the way of free delivery of goods, and for a time did an excellent business; but I came in competition with the great "Fruit House," the proprietor of which, being a heavy capitalist, could sell cheaper than I could buy. This hard rivalry discouraged me, and about the same time I was in failing health, being troubled with an affection of the heart. I applied to a physician for treatment and he prescribed whisky as a tonic. Previous to this, in all my experience, I had never tasted a drop of liquor in any form. I went to a drug store, purchased the whisky, and began taking it out of a spoon, as medicine only. It had a stimulating effect upon me, and made me feel better. I was greatly strengthened and my appetite was restored. In less than three months I was drinking it freely out of a jug. I soon formed an appetite for it; an appetite which adhered to me for many years, but which I finally, through the grace of God, was enabled to shake off.

It was at the " Lodge " saloon, in Fort Wayne, that I took my first glass of liquor over a bar. Well do I remember a cold winter day in 1866, when John Sterling, one of the proprietors, to whom I shall frequently refer, called me in and rallied me upon my delicate health. He said I ought to use liquor, and I swallowed his prescription without hesitation. From that time until a year ago I was addicted to the constant use of spirits. I believe that whisky benefited me when I first took it, but that it ever afterward proved a curse to me, and that, had I not abandoned its use in the nick of time, it would would have hurried me into a drunkard's grave.

Since leaving the army I had never touched a card or gambled in any form. One Sabbath I was standing in front of my store when I was accosted by one of my best customers—a prominent citizen and a man of high standing—who asked me to accompany him to the private room of a business man on Columbia street, to witness a "gentleman's game of poker." I consented and soon found myself and my companion engaged in the game. I lost all the money I had—sixty-seven dollars—and my associate was relieved of nearly one hundred dollars. We left and met again on the succeeding Tuesday evening, when I had expected to be initiated into a Masonic lodge. I dreaded the ordeal which I supposed awaited me and therefore concluded not to go to the lodge room. Instead, I went back to the "business man's" poker game on Columbia street, with the friend above referred to, and that night lost three hundred dollars more. From this moment the old love of play was aroused in my bosom, and soon acquired a complete mastery over me. I visited the "gentleman's game" at every opportunity, and in less than eighteen months had lost thirty-five hundred dollars in playing against it. By reason of my drinking and gambling, together with the severe competition I have referred to, my business was constantly falling off, and my finances had become very low. I sent to Geneseo for the money which I had there, stating that I needed it to enlarge my business. Of course it went the same old way, into the pockets of the gamblers. I finally discovered that the crowd of supposed "business men" who had been defeating me so badly at poker, were in fact expert, professional gamblers, one of them being the veteran sport, Capt. Phillips of Toledo, who afterwards died at Lima, Ohio.

Fort Wayne at that time was a paradise for gamblers and confidence men. The times were flush; money was plenty, and the spirit of speculation was rife. Fort Wayne, being an important railroad point, was a natural rendezvous for gamblers from all directions. They congregated here from New York, Chicago, Detroit, Cincinnati, St. Louis, Indianapolis, Cleveland, Canada, etc., and some of the largest games in the United States were maintained. The "Lodge" saloon to which I have referred, was one of the most famous resorts in the country. It was kept by John Sterling and William Grunauer, two men of extended reputation in the sporting fraternity. Mr. Sterling was a thorough gambler; a good-natured, warm-hearted man, always ready to help the needy or "skin a sucker." Mr. Grunauer was a cool-headed player, and had always been very successful. Their faro game was in full blast, and hundreds of dollars changed hands there nightly. Frequently the game ran up into the thousands, and during its existence, I presume at least a million of dollars was lost and won upon it.

Another great resort was the keno-rooms of Tim McCarthy, the noted billiardist, and champion of the State of Indiana. This game was carried on for about three years, during which time the proprietor netted at least twenty thousand dollars from it. Among its patrons were many of our most prominent business men. Keno is not a gambler's game; it is played mostly by amateurs, who do not stop to think that it is a certainty for them to lose. When it is considered that the banker does not wager a cent, but upon every game takes ten per cent. of the money invested, it will be seen that the players have no chance to win in the long run. The game is played with cards having several rows of numbers across them; corresponding numbers are placed upon ivory balls, which are deposited in a globe, from which they are withdrawn one at a time and the number called. As fast as the figures are called, the player deposits a button upon the corresponding number on his card, if it is there. The first player who gets a straight row of five buttons wins the game. The cards usually sell for from one dollar upwards, and the winner takes the proceeds after the percentage of the bank is withdrawn. At McCarthy's room these cards frequently sold as high as twenty dollars each, when the game was reduced to professional gamblers, making a pool of two hundred or three hundred dollars for the winner of a single game.

In 1866 and 1867 Fort Wayne was noted, not only as a gambling town, but as the headquarters of as desperate and skillful a gang of three-card monte men, pickpockets, and confidence men as could be found in the country. This gang was thoroughly organized, and numbered about thirty of the most expert operators in the United States. Their leader was Edward Ryan, who achieved a wide notoriety as the king of confidence men. For several years he and his *pals* carried things with a high hand in Fort Wayne. They exercised a potent influence in local politics, being feared by the politicians; and through their lavish expenditures of their ill-gotten plunder, gained a tacit support from many merchants and business men, who profited from their patronage.

This organization of thieves committed their principal depredations on the Pittsburgh, Fort Wayne & Chicago Railway, between Valparaiso and Lima, and the Wabash Railway, between Fort Wayne and Peru. Near the depot, in Fort Wayne, they carried on a saloon which was provided with secret rooms, trap doors, etc. In that hell many a poor fellow has been drugged and robbed of his last penny. They resorted to all kinds of expedients to raise the wind, from the simple picking of pockets, up to the most cleverly contrived and skillfully executed confidence games. They realized many thousands of dollars, which they squandered very freely, in gambling and extravagance. In the Fall of 1865, when the State Fair was held in Fort Wayne, they reaped a rich harvest. About thirty thousand people attended, and many of them fell into the hands of these Philistines. They operated with wonderful boldness and cunning. When a train arrived in the city, several of the thieves would jump into the cars, and begin picking pockets. As fast as they finished a man, they would chalk a cross upon his coat, so that the "boys" would waste no time upon him. The pocket-books would not be examined, but would be handed to confederates, who would hasten away with them. These accomplices would "skin the leathers" (take the money from the wallets), and then throw the empty purses on the roof of a shed at the rear of the robbers' saloon. To show how extensive these depredations were, it may be stated that at the end of the Fair week these pocket-books were gathered together and buried by one of the understrappers, and that they filled a bushel basket. He examined them and found sixty dollars in money, which had escaped observation. During this week the Ryan gang cleared many thousands of dollars.

"Competition is the life of trade," as a usual thing, but Ed. Ryan did not appreciate rivalry in his line of business. He claimed a monopoly of Fort Wayne and the railroads centering there, and would not brook any competition if he could avoid it. Once he was considerably alarmed by the arrival of Dennis Marks, a notorious confidence man from Chicago, who came with a party of kindred spirits for the purpose of harvesting in the field which he (Ryan) claimed as peculiarly his own. Ryan determined to drive the Marks crowd from the city, and found it necessary to resort to strategy in order to carry out his purpose. So he and an accomplice, known as "Hoosier Brown," perfected a scheme to disgust Marks, and it worked most admirably. One winter's afternoon Ryan invited Marks to take a sleigh ride, and the latter accepted. The pair drove toward the county asylum, when they met an old battered up specimen of humanity, trudging along in the snow, carrying a satchel. "There comes a good 'bloak,'" whispered Ryan. "Let's tackle him," said the Chicago sharper; and stopping the sleigh, they accosted the pedestrian:

"Hallo, stranger, where d'ye come from?"

"Wall, I kum from out south hyar, where I jes' sold my farm, and I kind u' thut as how I d go out nuth u' town a few miles, and buy 'nuther un, specially as I've got ther cash muney right here (tapping the satchel) to pay for it."

At this, Marks' eyes glistened. He invited the farmer to jump into the cutter and ride to town. The three went to the St. Nicholas saloon, where a drink was had all around. Marks then attempted to swindle the supposed greenhorn with the lock game. Ed. Ryan pretended to assist him. Marks closed the lock, and bet the stranger one thousand three hundred dollars that he couldn't unlock it. The latter, after some discussion, took the bet, and the money was placed in the hands of Hugh Doty, the bartender. The intended victim readily opened the lock, and immediately grabbed the two thousand six hundred dollars, and started for the door. He (the supposed intended dupe) had been playing the lock game himself, and was prepared to beat it when necessary.

"Stop that bloak; he's got my sugar," cried Marks, as he started in pursuit, whereupon Hoosier Brown, for it was he, drew a navy revolver, pointed it at the head of the Chicago thief and said:

"That money's mine. I won it and propose to keep it. D'ye hear."

Marks heard, and realized that he himself was the victim of a sharp confidence operation by Ryan and Brown. The latter walked off with his one thousand three hundred dollars, and Marks and his crony speedily left for Chicago, satisfied that Fort Wayne was no place for them.

The continued depredations of these confidence men, and their immunity from punishment, at last awakened public sentiment. The railroads passing through Fort Wayne experienced a heavy falling off in travel, because passengers would avoid these lines if possible. The companies employed detectives, but they accomplished little, but finally an incident occurred which led to the complete overthrow of the horde who had so long been undisturbed in their nefarious operations. Ryan succeeded in robbing an old man named Tucker from Columbia City, but Tucker was not made of the stuff of which most victims are composed, and pursued Ryan into the saloon with a revolver. The thief attempted to escape when Tucker fired at him, the ball striking his collar button and then glancing off, thus saving his life. Ryan was captured and taken to the police station, where a large crowd gathered that night for the purpose of inflicting summary justice. The desperado was well guarded, however, and the mob, composed mainly of shop men, satisfied themselves with burning down the saloon which had so long served as headquarters of the gang. Ryan succeeded in getting bail which he "jumped" and fled to Canada. He was afterwards captured, but escaped. He was re-captured and again escaped. He was secured a third time and brought to Fort Wayne for trial. He secured a change of venue, and was tried at Wabash, where he was convicted and sentenced to two years in the penitentiary. He served his sentence, after which he was a wanderer over the earth until his death, which occurred a few months ago in Chicago. The gang dispersed when their leader was apprehended, and their chosen resort was given over to the flames. Most of them are dead, several having expired in prison, and others having met violent ends— fitting climaxes to their desperate and lawless careers.

From the time that the confidence men deserted Fort Wayne, this city began to lose its prominence as a gambling center. These thieves had lost a large part of their booty to the professional sports, and when they departed, the gamblers found themselves short of victims. The thieves robbed the greenhorns, and in turn lost their "swag" at the faro bank or the poker table, taking to the road as soon as they were "broke" for the purpose of replenishing their exchequer. Those were indeed "lively times" in Indiana.

CHAPTER IV.

HOW I DEGENERATED FROM A BUSINESS MAN INTO A PROFESSIONAL GAMBLER — SEVERE LESSONS AT MY NEW TRADE — MY SAD EXPERIENCE AS MANAGER OF A MINSTREL TROUPE AND PROPRIETOR OF A VARIETY THEATER AT LAFAYETTE — UPS AND DOWNS AS A GAMBLER — A FARO GAME STOPPED BY A FEARFUL POWDER EXPLOSION.

The taste I had got of playing seemed to have aroused all my passion for this vice, which had lain dormant for a few months. I sought every opportunity to repair my losses, and satisfy the fondness I had for gaming. I was an habitual visitor to McCarthy's keno rooms, although I knew as well as I know now that I had a dead certainty of losing at that game; but I could not resist the fascination. I also got to visiting Sterling and Grunauer's faro bank over the "Lodge" and there I dropped many dollars.

I finally found that I could not be a gambler and a business man at the same time. As my trade had vanished and my reputation was clouded, I concluded to be a sport, out and out, and disposed of my grocery store for eight hundred and sixty-eight dollars. I then had my first experience as a faro dealer. I thought I understood the game, but in less than an hour after I opened the "bank" I had lost eight hundred dollars. The "sharks" as the outside players are called, had "goosed my kit;" *i. e.*, they had secured access to my tools and had tampered with them in such a way that they had a sure thing to win, while I had no possible chance. There are many ways of "goosing a kit," and gamblers are always striving to invent some new method of getting a dead sure thing on the game. If I had been an expert—if I had learned my trade, so to speak—I would have detected the scheme before putting the cards into the box. The cards had been sandpapered, and a genuine sport would have noticed it.

I had learned a lesson, however, and determined to profit by it. I joined the "sharks," or "rounders," and for some time played against the banks. I was learning "the ropes," and "stood in" with many schemes of "snaking the kits." Sometimes they succeeded, and sometimes they failed. Finally I obtained a stake, and opened a faro game, in a room over the Occidental Billiard Hall, in Fort Wayne. The sharks determined to "give it to me," and having made keys to fit the locks, bribed my room boy to give them access to my tools. He allowed them to do so, and they proceeded to "doctor" my cards, by punching small holes in them. After this was done, the boy told me what had been going on. I examined the cards, found the holes, and filled them up with white putty. That evening I opened the game just as if nothing had happened. A large number were present, and they evidently expected a "rich haul." I gave them all a chance to bet, and finally began dealing. Soon they all centered to one spot, the turn was made, and it "threw them." They looked at me and then at each other in blank amazement. None of them dared to speak, lest he expose the crowd. I acted as if nothing had happened, and did not seem to notice the quandary of the players. The scene was a comical one. I resumed dealing, and the next time there was a white show on top, they "bounced it," and lost again. Many a heavy sigh was drawn, and some of the lighter weights drew out, being short of funds. Their mouths were closed, but their looks and actions spoke louder than words. The game continued, and upon the next turn the " rounders " won. This was not surprising as I had no advantage, as the case stood. The last winning renewed the confidence of my antagonists. They evidently imagined that there had been some miscalculation on their part, but now they were certain, and they piled up their money. I let them crowd the limits, and upon the next turn they lost again. This finished them; the crowd was broke. They "squealed" and "kicked" terribly, and asked to see the cards, thus exposing their own plot. They examined the cards, and saw just how they had been "taken in, and done for." They "played for even," but could not make it. The best joke of the whole transaction, was that my partner "stood in" with the outside, trying to break me, and that he got a large and bitter dose of the medicine himself.

I continued dealing without any incident worthy of note until the Spring of 1868, when I found myself ashore, financially, and obtained a position to travel for J. C. Kennedy, of Chicago, and sell soda fountains. I was thus employed during most of the summer, spending my leisure time and spare change at the gambling table. In the Fall of that year, while at Kendallville, Ind., I made the acquaintance of a man named McCoole, who was traveling with a small tent show. This was during the political campaign, and McCoole was giving performances at the dates and places of the joint discussions between Governors Hendricks and Baker. He had been doing a good business, and at his solicitation I took a half interest in the show. The great Mason-McCoole prize fight had just taken place, and we named our troupe the Mason-McCoole Minstrels. We gave two performances each day — one in the afternoon in the tent, and one in the evening at a hall. We showed at Kendallville, Waterloo, and other points. From the latter place I went to Toledo with four hundred and fifty dollars in my pocket, to engage "talent" for our "mammoth combination" (as we called it on the bills); but instead of doing so, I fell against a faro bank at Toledo and lost every cent of it. I returned and joined the company. We played at Mishawakee to a fair business, and then proceeded to South Bend, where we rented a hall and announced a grand musical entertainment. The evening came, and so did the crowd. We had a large attendance, our receipts being about one hundred and fifty dollars. McCoole was in the box office selling tickets, and I stood at the door. About eight o'clock, just before time for the curtain to raise, my partner told me he was going down stairs for a moment, and said that I should take in money at the door until his return. I stood there and received about two dollars and a half in "shinnies" (fractional currency). It was past the time for the curtain to raise, and the audience were becoming impatient. About this time the owner of the hall arrived and demanded his rent. I told him McCoole had gone out with all of the funds, and asked him to wait until his return. He respectfully declined, and said the curtain should not go up until the money was paid. I argued with him, and offered him as security the canvas which we had purchased from Gilbert & Grady for one hundred dollars. He was obdurate, evidently believing that McCoole and myself were in complicity for the purpose of defrauding him. My position was indeed an embarrassing one. I had only two dollars and a half in money, was an entire stranger, and had to face an angry audience. I finally mounted the stage, and told the crowd the circumstances. I said that we were ready to proceed if the owner of the hall would let us, and concluded by throwing my scrip and tickets among the audience. They were very indignant, and I feared that they would use violence with me. They left the hall pell-mell, with many expressions of anger and disgust. The members of the company — none of whom had been paid for a long time — were uneasy at the turn affairs had taken, and thought that their private property would be attached. One of them owned a banjo which he valued at one hundred dollars, and he was determined to save it at all hazards. Sending a confederate to the front of the building, he let down the banjo from the window with a string, crying to a man below, " Is that you, Jake ? " " Yes," was the answer, and the instrument was let down into the hands of the — sheriff. That was the last seen of that banjo. This incident confirmed the belief that we were attempting a deliberate swindle, although the only guilty party was McCoole. He had boarded a train and left the city, and from that day to this I have never seen or heard of him.

I was left in South Bend with ten unpaid performers on my hands, without money or friends, and with a number of bills to settle. I went to the hotel, and turned over the canvas to the landlord as security for our bill. I presume he has the canvas yet. We slept at the hotel, but were refused breakfast the next morning, and left the hotel hungry and broke. A thorough search was made of every member of the troupe, and finally we succeeded in discovering a dollar bill concealed in the watch pocket of one of the players. That was promptly confiscated and devoted to the purchase of a lunch. The company disbanded, each person depending upon his wits to get out of town.

I then formed a partnership with a fortune teller whose acquaintance I had made, and we proceeded to Kendallville, and then to Fort Wayne, my fare and expenses being paid by my new companion. At the latter place the fortune teller located at the Hedekin House, remaining three weeks, telling no less than two hundred and fifty fortunes, at one dollar each, within that time. This large business was the result of liberal advertising, and the success with which the past and present of the "seekers after knowledge" were told. This seemed remarkable, and was the subject of much amazement among the simple-minded persons who paid their dollars for a knowledge of the future. There was nothing supernatural, however, about the success with which "fortunes" were told. I was getting half of the profits, and, in order to earn my way, made myself an active assistant. I knew almost all who went to have their fortunes told, and during the operation I was concealed behind a door, sharing my knowledge with the professor of occult mysteries. The victim was always placed with his back toward me. Thus, if the party was married, I nodded my head; if single, I shook my head; I signified the number of children he or she had by my fingers, and in various ways I gave information which, when imparted by the fortune teller, produced the greatest surprise and wonderment. Such of my young readers as may feel tempted to consult these so-called "oracles" will see, from my narrative, that there is no reliance to be placed in them, and that, when they do tell the truth, it is either the result of a lucky guess, or of knowledge obtained in some manner not suspected by the victim.

When our business became dull at Fort

Wayne, we went to Huntington, and there, for obvious reasons, our success was not so great. We dissolved partnership, the fortune teller leaving for parts unknown. Sterling and Grunauer were running a faro bank at Huntington, and they employed me to deal at eight dollars per day. They were in bad luck, and, having lost eighteen hundred dollars, closed the faro bank and left for Fort Wayne. In the mean time I had gambled away all my profits from the fortune telling, and returned home.

I then obtained the money due me for selling soda fountains, amounting to seven hundred dollars. Of course the first thing I did was to seek a gambling room, and on Sunday night I found myself at the "Lodge." When I arose from the faro table that night, I did not have money enough to buy a cigar with, and was at a loss to imagine what to do next.

The next morning I was sitting in the "Lodge" trying to invent some means of "raising the wind," when I happened to think of a man in Lafayette, to whom I had loaned one hundred and ninety dollars, and who was about leaving for the Far West. I determined to go to Lafayette to see him, but how to get there was the question. I asked Grunauer—one of the men who had won my seven hundred dollars the preceding evening—for a small loan, but he refused unless I would put up a gold elephant as security. From his partner, Sterling, I met with better treatment. He advised me not to get discouraged, and when I stated my case handed me twenty dollars with which I went to Lafayette, arriving there with sixteen dollars. The man who owed me one hundred and ninety dollars had departed. I was about leaving for home, when I met one of the former members of the defunct " Mason-McCoole Minstrels." He was performing at a variety theater in Lafayette, the proprietor of which was losing money and was anxious to sell out. At his suggestion I purchased the establishment, giving my notes for three hundred and fifty dollars at three and six months' time. I went to Indianapolis, engaged the Reynard sisters who were billed as "celebrated *artistes*," and I soon had my variety hell in full blast. It was located at No. 54 Fourth street, and will doubtless be remembered by many of the citizens of Lafayette as one of the hardest places ever kept in that city. I fitted up a bar, a green-room, and all the other adjuncts of a place of this character, and did a thriving business. The place was crowded every night. I changed the company every two or three weeks and employed a large number of " gifted stars " to cater to the tastes of my patrons. The green-room was conducted on the most approved principles. I bought wine at thirty-seven and a-half cents a bottle and sold it for two dollars and fifty cents. The "lady performers" received fifteen dollars a week each, and board, together with fifty cents commission for each bottle of wine sold. Strange to say, among the persons who paid two dollars and fifty cents per bottle for this wine, were the men from whom I had bought it for thirty-seven and a half cents.

I charged an admission fee of twenty-five cents, each check calling for a glass of beer. This was done in order to avoid payment of license.

My variety hall gradually became the rendezvous of disorderly characters and a nuisance in the eyes of decent citizens.

After I had conducted it about eight months, a determined attempt was made to break it up. Nearly one hundred indictments were returned against me, but owing to legal irregularities and a failure of proof, I had them quashed at an expense of only five dollars, which I paid an attorney. I concluded that it was about time for me to remove, so I decided to shut up. Owing to a misunderstanding with the gas company, the theater was lighted with thirty tallow candles at the last performance, and resembled an Irish wake in appearance. The next day I closed the place, leaving stage, scenery, chairs, bar, etc., turned the key over to the owner of the building, and withdrew from the amusement business.

I can truthfully say that among the many regrettable episodes in my past life, there is none I look back upon with more sorrow and remorse than the one I have just related. I believe—and with my experience I certainly know whereof I speak—that of all the devil's inventions for propagating vice and dissipation, and leading young men into paths of immorality and indulgence, there are none more successful than "variety theaters" and "concert halls." They are perfect plague spots, full of evil and nothing but evil. The young man who frequents them is treading the path to certain ruin, and I warn all who do not desire to become moral wrecks, to avoid these places as they would a pestilence. Wherever they are established they do an amount of mischief which no one can estimate. I regret to say that they are frequently patronized and encouraged by business men who have sons and daughters growing up, and who are to a large extent responsible for their existence. I think the press and the pulpit, and an enlightened public sentiment, should unite to render the maintenance of such places of resort impossible.

When I closed my variety theater, I had sixteen hundred dollars in my pocket, the profits of that enterprise. It is needless to say that this money lasted me but a short time. I went to Chicago, and a very few contests with faro reduced me to pauperism. I then returned to Fort Wayne, after an absence of nearly a year, and rented a small room over the "Occidental," paying sixty dollars a month rent, and having borrowed a little money, opened a faro game on a light scale. I opened a "fifteen dollar snap," (the bets being limited to that amount) and at the first sitting won one hundred and ninety-five dollars. I had a streak of "good luck," and for six weeks never suffered a single loss amounting to a hundred dollars. I had then gathered forty-eight hundred dollars. I hired a dealer with whom I left a "bank roll" and two five hundred dollar bank checks, to be used in an emergency. I then started for Indianapolis, but had hardly reached there when I received a telegram to come home. Upon my return I discovered that my game had lost twelve hundred dollars. The dealer whom I had employed and trusted had played false with me, and by complicity with outsiders, had robbed me of the amount named. He was at once set down by the Fort Wayne gambling fraternity as a thief, and having lost the money he stole from me, as a "rounder" on outside games, he found the atmosphere very uncongenial, and left for parts unknown. I continued my game over the "Occidental" until my money had vanished, and I was compelled to close the bank and vacate my rooms.

After this I remained on the "ragged edge," financially, for several months. I played on the "outside," occasionally borrowing a small "stake," and making small winnings, which were lost upon the next game. Finally I borrowed five hundred dollars of a friend and opened a faro bank on Main Street. I had bad luck, and was cleaned out immediately. I obtained two hundred and fifty dollars more of the same man, which went after the five hundred dollars, and again he advanced me two hundred and fifty dollars, which also vanished. A fourth time I applied to him, but he could only let me have ten dollars; with this we went on a spree. I remained drunk constantly for weeks, both night and day, living on plain whisky, and taking but little food or sleep. Completely worn out, I finally sobered up. I was, of course, out of funds, and my debts amounted to about two thousand three hundred dollars. In order to get a start, I pawned an old watch for fifty-five dollars, and opened a game. By some means a rumor that I had won one thousand dollars, obtained circulation among the sports, and I took no pains to stop it, as I knew it would bring players against my bank. Luck had at last turned. The first night I dealt I won three hundred and sixty-five dollars. I kept on winning, and in less than three weeks I had paid all my debts and had a "bank roll" (business capital) of eight hundred dollars. As usual when successful I took to drinking, and my pile began to dwindle. Then I allowed outsiders to deal "snaps" (limited bets) at my game, and I played against them, usually winning, as few of them knew how to protect themselves.

At this time I was dividing my attention about equally between drinking and gambling. While on a spree, I went to Upper Sandusky, Ohio, leaving my rooms and a bank roll of four hundred dollars with my dealer. At Upper Sandusky I met some boon companions, and indulged in a frightful debauch. One day, as I was sleeping off the effects of this indulgence, under a large sycamore tree at the river side, I was handed a telegram, summoning me home. I returned to Fort Wayne and found my game broken up and my money gone.

I remained quiet for a few weeks, and then re-opened my old rooms over the "Occidental." Fortune again smiled upon me; and in about seven weeks my net winnings amounted to over four thousand dollars. During this time I had remained sober, watched my game, and had not made a single losing of any consequence. This was entirely too much prosperity for me to stand. I came to the conclusion that I must have a horse, and I bought a trotter for one hundred and ninety dollars, purchased a nobby wagon at Detroit, and made my appearance with a flashy turnout. I entered my horse at the Huntington Fair, and carried off the prize in the "general purposes" class. For a few weeks I devoted myself entirely to my horse and to drinking. Almost every day I became intoxicated and drove out, scarcely ever returning, unless my recklessness had caused some accident. Frequently I landed the whole turnout in the ditch, and rarely went to the stable with a whole wagon.

Laboring under the delusion that I had a fast trotter, I matched him against a better horse for two hundred dollars a side, and we had a trot on the snow, near the city. I of course came out second best, and finding I was beat did not stop, but drove straight to town, leaving a crowd of disgusted sports, who had bet on me, far in the rear. This was known as the "Birdie" and "Flossy" race.

The large sum of money, which I had recently won, had about disappeared, and in order to get another start, I sold my rig at a great sacrifice, and invested the proceeds in faro. Of course I lost, and I found myself, as I had so often been before — penniless.

MASON LONG'S FARO ROOM RAIDED BY THE POLICE, AT FORT WAYNE, INDIANA.

In the Spring of 1871, I obtained a small stake and opened a faro bank in the third story of the building at the corner of Calhoun and Wayne Streets, Fort Wayne. There was no other game in the city at the time, and this one was well patronized. A great many transient sports visited Fort Wayne those days and they, together with merchants, bankers, saloon-keepers, clerks, bartenders, railroad conductors, etc., composed the players. Occasionally a church member dropped in and took a hand. Among all of the players, passenger conductors and bartenders were the hardest for us to keep broke. Many saloon-keepers visited us once or twice a week, and left with us, for safe keeping, all their available cash. The game kept up remarkably well, hundreds of dollars changing hands every night.

While I was conducting this bank, an incident took place which is, I think, worth relating. One night in June, 1871, I was dealing and there was an exciting game in progress for " big money." Suddenly we discovered a bright light in our windows, and soon became aware that fire was raging in the adjoining building. The steam engines were throwing water on the fire, and we could hear the noise of the large crowd which had assembled in the street below, and the shrill voices of the firemen and policemen as they moved about in the discharge of their duties. The game was kept up as if nothing had happened; not a player rose from his seat, not a man passed in his checks, so engrossing was the sport. It was suggested that we would not move until the walls grew hot, and we kept on dealing and playing, with the adjacent building in flames. It was not until an explosion took place, which shook the edifice from foundation to roof, that some of the players became terrified, drew out of the game and left. I continued dealing, however, and scarcely a word was spoken as the game progressed, although the roar from the street below was becoming louder and louder. In a few moments a second violent explosion occurred which moved the building several inches, shattered every window in our room to fragments, lifted the door from its hinges and overturned the check rack. This made the stoutest heart fail, and the most hardened countenances blanch. We feared that the stairway had been torn away, and all egress cut off, and the reckless men, who had been tempting fate, forgetting everything, rushed for the exit. No one waited to get his checks cashed, and I never closed a game more suddenly. The stairways were all right and we soon reached the street. We found that the fire had originated in the cellar beneath Boltz's grocery in the adjacent building. The first shock was caused by the explosion of some oil in the cellar, which had been afterward flooded with water. The boiling oil ran along the surface of the water and generated gas. When Fred. Hilsmau, a torch boy, entered the cellar, this gas exploded with a loud report, killing him instantly and wounding about twenty-five persons. Mr. Ferd. Boltz, proprietor of the grocery; Thomas Mannix, the Chief Engineer of the Fire Department; John Downey and Edward Downey were among those most frightfully burned. Their sufferings were most intense, and they presented as horrible a spectacle as I ever witnessed during the war. We gamblers devoted the remainder of the night to caring for the wounded, who were removed to hospitals and private residences. This striking episode was a great shock to all of us, and we did not recover from its effects for some time.

CHAPTER V.

THE HORRORS OF DELIRIUM TREMENS—VISIONS OF THE "WHITE MICE"—REPEATED CAPTURES BY THE POLICE—LUDICROUS FLIGHT OF A BLOODTHIRSTY SPORT—LARGE WINNINGS INVESTED IN A PALATIAL SALOON AND GAMBLING DEN—RECKLESS DISSIPATION AND PRODIGALITY—AN HOUR IN JAIL—LOW EBB OF FORTUNE.

I was completely unnerved by the terrible event which I described in the concluding pages of the last chapter. I did not make a single winning for at least a month. I was extremely nervous whenever I sat down at a card table. Becoming discouraged, I betook myself to my usual resort, the bottle, and indulged in a prolonged spree. For many days I subsisted almost entirely upon raw whisky, sleeping but little, and eating scarcely anything. At last I found myself suffering from my first attack of *delirium tremens*. My visions assumed the forms of white mice. They were ever before my eyes, waking or sleeping. They were constantly present in my diseased imagination, crawling over my bed at night, swarming about my person by day, advancing toward me in vast multitudes, crawling about my feet with every step. In vain did I attempt to shake off this dreadful vagary; with every effort the white mice increased in numbers, until it seemed to me that thousands of them were about me, and that I would never be able to free myself from them. They seemed within my reach, but when I clutched at them they evaded my hands, and seemed to laugh demoniacally at my fruitless attempts to capture them. My physical condition was pitiable; I was pale, weak, nervous, exhausted, unable to collect my thoughts, or control my fancies. I slowly recovered from this attack, but it was many weeks before I regained my usual life, energy, and buoyant spirits. Thoroughly frightened at last, I determined to stop drinking, and for four months did not touch a drop.

When I "got on my feet again," I opened a faro bank in the old rooms previously occupied by Sterling and Grunauer. The game flourished, and for about three months I won steadily. One night there was a big game in progress, many prominent sporting men from abroad being present and playing against me, when a *posse* of police suddenly made their appearance, entering through the skylight and the rear windows, which they had reached by means of a ladder. The game was intensely exciting, and we did not hear the approach of the "peelers." Our first intimation that they were in the vicinity, was when they stood before us and told us to consider ourselves under arrest. The countenances of the eighteen players in the room were indeed a study, and presented a ludicrous spectacle. This raid was the immediate result of the threats made by one of the number, who had threatened publicly to kill the first "peeler" who should ever attempt his arrest in a gambling room. This threat nettled the bold chief, "Mike" Singleton, who laid his plans carefully to "bag" this dangerous (?) sport. The raid was cleverly executed, and, as was to be expected, the valor of the sanguinary individual referred to, rapidly oozed out at the pores. In the confusion, he entered my sleeping apartment and locked the door. The police attempted to force it open, but I warned them not to do so, as the room was a private one, not used for gambling purposes. They allowed us to settle up the game, and then confiscated my tools, and marched us to the lock-up. As we reached the hallway, the cowardly braggadocio who had locked himself in my bedroom opened the door, dashed through the gambling hall, and jumped out of the back window, taking sash and all with him. He landed in a garden, and thus made good his escape, as the police could not leave us to look after him.

I had won five hundred dollars before the raid, but had to deposit one hundred and eighty dollars to secure the release of the crowd, and in the bargain, lost my kit of checks, valued at one hundred dollars.

Of course, these police raids were of more or less frequent occurrence. During my ten years of gambling in Fort Wayne, my house was "pulled," on an average, two or three times annually. I never allowed any man caught in my place to be locked up, even if I had to borrow money to bail him out with. I presume I have paid into the city treasury of Fort Wayne, in consequence of these arrests, not less than two thousand five hundred or three thousand dollars, not to speak of the loss I sustained by the confiscation of many valuable kits of tools.

The newspapers and the public generally are in the habit of censuring police officers for the infrequency of their raids upon gamblers, and in many cases, without reason. It is a most difficult matter to make these arrests successfully. The police have no right to break into a room upon suspicion, merely, and they do so at their own risk. In order to work a conviction, it is necessary to prove the gambling, and that is very frequently hard to do, as, in many cases, it could only be done through the testimony of the players themselves, and no one can be required to criminate himself on the witness stand. Many skillfully planned and cleverly executed raids have proved "water hauls," merely because the officers were unable to show positively that gambling was being done. The doors are always kept locked and bolted, with a guard outside to give warning, by an understood signal, of the approach of the "cops." It is an easy thing to secrete and lock up cards, tools, etc., and by the time the officers gain admission—if they do so at all—they frequently find only a party of gentlemen quietly smoking cigars and reading the newspapers. The officers have no right to break open trunks, or closets, upon suspicion that they contain gambling tools, and, in such cases, it is useless to make arrests.

I have known the police to work for weeks devising some plan of bagging a nest of sports. They usually choose a time when the gamblers are supposed to be "flush," in order that the city treasury may receive a "benefit." They scale buildings, climb ladders, let themselves down from the roofs through skylights, disguise themselves in citizen's clothes, and, in fact, resort to all manner of stratagems to capture the gentlemen who buck the tiger.

Of course, there are many ludicrous incidents connected with these affairs. One night, while I was keeping a room at 74 Calhoun Street, Fort Wayne, the "peelers" stealthily crept up to our outside guard, who was sitting in front of the door asleep, seized him, and before he was fairly awake, had taken the keys from his pocket, and entered our room, much to our disgust and amazement; of course, we had to "walk up to the captain's office and settle."

Occasionally a man who never plays drops into a gambling room as a spectator, through mere curiosity. When such "innocents" find themselves in the hands of the police, their terror is very amusing to the thoroughbreds, who are hardened to such experiences. I remember distinctly the futile and ridiculous efforts of two of these "spring chickens" to escape from the blue coats in one of my Fort Wayne rooms, on West Berry Street. There was a small dumb waiter in the room, in which drinks and cigars were brought up from the saloon below. This was about large enough to hold a very small tray; but when the officers arrived that night, these two boys jumped into it and attempted to run it down. It is as hard for a camel to pass through the eye of a needle as it was for these worthies to descend through this small space; and as the police gently took them forth from their ridiculous hiding-place, their countenances presented a decidedly sheepish aspect. This was probably their first visit to a gambling room, and they had never played; but like the rest of us, they had to "plank down" ten dollars each. It was probably the best thing that

4*

could have happened them, as they doubtless concluded to keep out of such places in future.

One of my sporting enterprises in Fort Wayne was a private "club room" for gentlemen. This place was frequented by some of the leading business men and wealthiest citizens of Fort Wayne, who liked to play among themselves, but did not desire to come in contact with regular sporting men. They were bankers, capitalists, merchants, city and county officials, and men of that class. While I kept this room, the mayor received an anonymous letter, to the effect that it was resorted to by mechanics, laboring men, and others, who were there robbed of the money which their wives and children needed. Upon the strength of this, he ordered the chief of police to make an immediate raid, and to refuse less than fifty dollars bail in each case. And so we received a call one night, and the "peelers" found six of the leading citizens of Fort Wayne having a quiet game of poker among themselves. They were all put under arrest, but, of course, promptly furnished bail. One of the police "froze" to my check-rack, which I hated to part with. I tried to get it from him by various devices, which proved fruitless. Finally, as the police were about leaving, I invited them to "take something." The room-boy brought up a "round of drinks," and the "peeler" laid down my check-rack while he absorbed his liquor; when he had swallowed his drink, he reached for the "rack," but it was gone—safely lodged in a clothes-press, which was locked, and which the police dared not open. They could get no information as to the mysterious disappearance, and took their departure minus the trophy; the chief, in the meantime, administering a severe reprimand to the officer whose fondness for liquor had caused the trouble.

After our guests departed, we had another game, in which I won four hundred and twenty-five dollars from the business men, none of whom has probably forgotten this, to them, eventful night.

The "raid" which caused the bully to jump from the window, frightened the owner of the building, and he gave me notice to vacate. I then returned to the room which I had occupied at the time of the explosion. There were two faro banks in full blast in this building, one kept by a noted Louisville sport named Gregg, who afterwards died of small pox, and the other by myself. Business was good here, but I soon made another move to No. 60 Calhoun Street where I ran the largest game I ever had. During the races of 1872, there was "big money" lost against my game. In one night I won over twenty-two hundred and fifty dollars in two hours, of which seventeen hundred dollars was lost by Jesse Winter, a well-known gambler of Cincinnati, and four hundred dollars by a traveling salesman for an Indianapolis firm, who was shortly afterward sent to the penitentiary for embezzlement.

In the Spring of 1873, two men from Fort Wayne and myself opened a faro game at Logansport, where we speedily lost our bank roll of two thousand dollars. My partners returned to Fort Wayne for money, and during their absence, I borrowed two hundred dollars, and opened a two hundred dollar "snap." I won seven hundred dollars the first night, and when my partners got back had thirty-one hundred dollars. We re-opened our game with a nine hundred dollar bank roll, which disappeared the first two nights, whereupon my partners left in disgust. I remained in Logansport and dipped into a big game of poker at which I lost twenty-one hundred dollars in one week. I then resumed faro, and having won nine hundred dollars left for Fort Wayne with sixteen hundred dollars in my pocket.

I then determined to embark in the saloon business, and conduct a gambling room in connection therewith. I leased a building at No. 74 Calhoun Street in the Summer of 1873, and fitted it up at an expense of thirty-five hundred dollars, of which I paid sixteen hundred dollars in cash. The saloon, when thrown open, was the handsomest in the city. There was an elegant black walnut bar, a black walnut sideboard, costing five hundred dollars, mirrors, Brussels carpets, etc. The rooms were supplied with fine billiard tables which I purchased on time, giving my notes therefor, and afterward winning the notes from the holder at the gaming table.

I opened to an immense business. My predecessor at this place, took in only from three to eight dollars a day; but the first day I opened, my bar receipts were forty dollars, and they increased daily until they reached one hundred and seventy-five dollars. The first month my sales amounted to twenty-two hundred and fifty dollars for whisky, billiards, etc. My gambling rooms were in the second story, and business was so brisk that I had to have two kits and tables, and two games frequently running in one room. The first year, the entire institution, gambling room, saloon, etc., netted me over eight thousand dollars, and yet at its termination, I was fifteen hundred dollars in debt, all caused by recklessness, extravagance, and dissipation. During the Northern Indiana Fair of 1874, I reaped a rich harvest. I conducted a bar two hundred feet long at the Fair grounds, and on the day of the Firemen's Tournament, when there were said to have been forty thousand people on the grounds, the receipts were thirteen hundred and sixty-five dollars for beer, whisky, and cigars at this place. On the same day, the receipts at my saloon and gambling hall were fourteen hundred and fifty dollars, most of which was realized from the games. During these races, there were three games of faro and one "red and black table" in constant operation in my rooms.

Another profitable time for me was the great Soldiers Re-union of 1874, when my receipts were very large. Many of them dropped in to see me, and one night I won about nine hundred dollars from them, for *old acquaintance sake*.

These were the most profitable days, financially, I ever had, and yet they availed me little. I was constantly in debt, and squandered my money in all kinds of reckless dissipation and extravagance. My establishment being the headquarters of professional gamblers, attracted many loafers and hangers-on. This gradually drove away my best customers. I drank and caroused around freely, neglected my business, and let my stock run down. Whenever I got two thousand, three thousand, or four thousand dollars together, I left the city to attend horse races, chicken fights, or some other similar affair, and frequently returned without a cent.

I will describe one trip, as an illustration. In the Spring of 1874, I left home to attend a chicken fight, at Tolleston, Ind., the match being between the Chappell Brothers, of Detroit, and Jerry Monroe, of Chicago. I was on a spree when I left home, and took a bottle of whisky with me, from which I drank so freely that I was carried past Tolleston, and into Chicago, where I arrived in the morning. I stepped into a restaurant, took a cocktail, ordered breakfast, and while it was being prepared, went up stairs to visit a faro game; while my pheasant was being broiled, I won eight hundred and forty dollars, and when the bell rang for breakfast, I sat down with that amount of winnings in my pocket. I dropped into a pawn-shop, where I paid five hundred and twenty dollars for a watch and chain, and one hundred and forty five dollars for a pair of bracelets, for neither of which I had any use, and returned to Fort Wayne. I mention this simply as an illustration of the extravagance and recklessness of the average gambler. In three days after purchasing this watch and chain, I had it pawned for three hundred dollars.* I frequently had it in " soak " after that, and altogether I presume I borrowed not less than twenty-five hundred dollars upon it. I finally sacrificed it for one hundred and seventy dollars.

My palatial gambling room and saloon was rapidly becoming one of the worst dens in the city. That which I had originally intended as a resort for gentlemen and business men, became finally the headquarters of all the bleareyed bummers, whisky bloats, and dead-beats in the city. People with any claims to respectability, avoided it studiously. The newspapers "wrote it up," and facetiously denominated it "Mace Long's Bazaar," and "Mace Long's Confectionery." My game was deserted, I was out of funds, badly entangled in debt, and I gave myself up to the grossest intemperance.

About this time I employed an old soak known to local fame as "Deacon" Bronson, as my bartender. The Deacon was a "character." Once a prominent railroad man, afterward the proprietor of some of the most fashionable and popular drinking resorts in the city, the Deacon had gone down step by step, until he had become a mere common drunkard. His excessive use of liquor had softened a brain which had never, to tell the truth, been phenomenally developed; and the Deacon, was a target for all the corner loafers in town.

I employed the Deacon at a nominal salary, his board and liquor being the main inducements. His duties were not very arduous, but he exerted himself quite successfully to see that my stock of liquors did not accumulate too fast. The customers were quite scarce, and those who did call were usually out of funds.

One cold winter morning an event of unusual interest transpired. A customer called — a real customer, with a clean shirt on, and some money in his pocket. I had been absent for some time on a spree. The Deacon had just opened the saloon, and had searched in vain for his morning bitters, the stock of liquor being exhausted. He was standing behind the bar, rubbing his hands and looking decidedly uncomfortable, when the aforesaid stranger entered.

"Give me some whisky," said he.

"We haven't got any whisky this morning," drawled out the Deacon, rubbing his hands as before.

"Well, give me some beer, then."

"We haven't got any beer," again whimpered the Deacon, in his usual sing-song style, still rubbing his hands.

"Give me a cigar, then," was the next order.

"We haven't got any cigars," said the Deacon, as he rubbed his hands some more.

"What in h— have you got?" ejaculated the would-be customer, in disgust.

"We have some real nice claret wine," replied the Deacon, as he took another rub at his hands.

"D—d if I'll make an ice cream freezer out of my stomach such a day as this," was the final remark of the gentleman, as he passed out the door.

Claret, as the reader is aware, is a summer drink, and is as much out of place on a cold winter's day as ice cream or soda water.

I arrived at the saloon shortly afterward, learned the situation, and concluded to stock up. I handed my able assistant ninety cents, and with that amount he visited the Fruit House, purchased a gallon of the "best imported liquor," and when he returned we were again ready for business. The Deacon took care that the whisky should not spoil.

About this time I made a desperate attempt to retrieve my failing fortunes. I sold off my billiard tables to citizens for their private residences. I converted my establishment into a beer saloon, with waiter girls as attractions. This expedient revived business temporarily, but trade soon dropped off again. My institution was more of a nuisance than ever, for there are few greater pests in a city than these waiter-girl saloons.

About this time some of my creditors became impatient with me, brought suits, and obtained judgments. Executions were issued against me, and one night at a late hour a constable entered my saloon for the purpose of making a levy. I was drunk, and was sitting at a beer table with a couple of boon companions, who were in the same condition. The constable was at least as drunk as I. When he served the execution I said I would lock up, and give him the keys until the next morning, when I would raise the money and pay the judgment. He told me to keep open and sell, and he would stay and take the money, to be applied in payment. I consented, and resumed my seat at the table, anxiously waiting for some customers. Soon I noticed the officer behind the bar dealing out the whisky and cigars to himself, and a crowd of his dead-beat associates. Of course I protested, whereupon he took hold of some furniture and began moving it out. Upon this I seized him by the neck and produced considerable pressure upon his windpipe. He then took his departure, threatening to return shortly.

I again seated myself with my two companions, and in a little while the enraged officer re-turned, entering through the back door which I had forgotten to lock. He tried to read the warrant, but was too drunk to do so. I consented to accompany him, however, and started out of the door with him. As we were leaving, my two *pals* showed their devotion to my cause by novel demonstrations, one of them giving the constable a terrible kick in an exposed portion of his anatomy, and the other placing the lighted end of a cigar gently against his neck. He uttered an exclamation of pain and hurried me before a magistrate, where I was ordered to give fifty dollars bonds for my appearance the next day, and being unable to do so was committed to jail. I walked over with the constable and when we entered the building I dealt him a vigorous blow in the head, laying him flat upon the stone floor. The turnkey seized me and hustled me into a cell. There were two horse thieves in the next cell and a murderer just above. I undressed, laid down on my bunk, and soon fell into a drunken slumber. In a short time I was awakened, two friends having come over and secured my release. Thus ended the only "half hour in jail" I ever passed.

The next day I raised the wind, paid my fine, and in the evening re-opened my faro bank with only seventy-five dollars on hand. I made some small winnings, but, convinced that it was useless to attempt longer to stem the tide, I therefore "locked myself up," *i. e.*, closed the saloon and disposed of it to the best advantage for the benefit of my creditors. The remnants of the establishment which had originally cost thirty-five hundred dollars sold for only four hundred and twenty-five dollars, and that amount I handed over to my creditors.

Then I was afloat again. The vice of intemperance had kept growing upon me and I was intoxicated most of the time. I opened a "gentleman's poker room," but scarcely any one visited it, and I was generally too drunk to attend to it; I was "going down hill" more rapidly than ever, and every one was ready, as usual, to give me a kick. I partially recovered myself, however, and returned to my former rooms at No. 60 Calhoun, where I carried on my game with varying fortune, until my conversion, a little more than a year after. Then I bade farewell forever to the vice which had kept me a slave for so many years, broke the bonds which had held me so tightly, and found peace and happiness in believing.

CHAPTER VI.

"FOLLOWING THE TROTTERS"—SIGHTS AND SCENES ON THE TURF—MAKE-SHIFTS OF A BROKEN GAMBLER— CANADA BILL'S CONFIDENCE OPERATIONS—TRAVEL- ING ON "CHEEK"—A FOURTEEN MONTHS' DEBAUCH— ANOTHER HORRIBLE EXPERIENCE WITH DELIRIUM TREMENS.

For eight years I made a practice of attending the horse-races throughout the country. I "followed the trotters" from State to State, partly for the sake of gambling on the races and partly in order to participate in the large games which were in full blast during these meetings. I was thus engaged for the greater part of every season, and in the course of these tours passed through many adventures, such as are incident to the career of a gambler; some of them will perhaps be found of interest to the reader.

My fortune in betting upon horses was almost invariably poor. I never was able to "get into the ring," unless it was one intended for my especial benefit, in order to rob me. Once in a great while, however, I had a small sized "streak of luck" in this line. Among the earliest meetings I attended was at Hunttington, a number of years ago. Eight horses were entered in one of the races, two of them going in the pools as favorites and the others selling as a "field." I did not know a horse in the race, and concluded to buy the "field," which I did in a great many pools, on the night before the race. When I arrived on the grounds I discovered that all the horses had been withdrawn, save three, and I loudly protested to the judges that they "couldn't make a field out of one old gray horse." But of course I was overruled, and the horses started. I tried to sell my pools for five dollars, but in vain, and held my tickets, as no one else would have them. In the first heat, however, one of the favorite horses was distanced for fear of a record. In the second the other was taken sick and drawn out, and this left the old gray to trot the race alone. I won a handsome amount, which I hastened to draw from the pool box; afterward the pools were declared "off," and I was besieged for the money, which I gently but firmly declined to pay over, to the disappointment of those who had bought the "favorites." Some of them threatened to "bend my nose for me;" consulting the dictates of prudence, I therefore hastened to town.

That night I engaged in a game of poker with a stranger—a keen, wary, quiet individual, with a deep, mysterious look in his small, piercing eyes —who raked in all of my winnings on the race. I was cheating in the game but got beaten every time. I could not understand this, until I was informed that my adversary had a machine in his coat sleeve by means of which he played a "sure thing" game. The sports were anxious to examine it, and that evening we got the stranger engaged in an interesting game of billiards, at which he was an expert. The boys made some bets, and the stranger, getting warmed up, drew off his coat in order to play better; while he was engrossed in the game, the boys purloined his coat, and took the machine out of the sleeve. When our new acquaintance discovered the trick which had been played upon him, he cried bitterly, saying he had studied three years to invent the contrivance, by means of which he had victimized me so cleverly, but it had never worked successfully until that day. It was what we called a "sleeve hold-out," and that was the first time it was ever played on the Wabash, although it afterward became very common. With my customary bad luck I was its first dupe.

Frequently while attending the races, in Indiana towns, I dealt faro, which is a popular game with those who delight in the turf. Once while visiting a fair at Goshen, I opened a bank in the basement of the Violett House, having a cash capital of only three dollars. I took my chances of winning, and risky ones they were. No man who has never been "behind the box" can realize the feelings of one who opens a game with little or no capital and expects to be "broke" at every turn. On the evening in question I sold one hundred dollars worth of checks before pulling a card, and started out with losses of two hundred and fifty dollars; at any moment the players were liable to present their checks, which I could not have redeemed, and if by this means they had discovered that they had been playing against nothing, their wrath would have been terrible.

I realized my situation, but continued dealing with plenty of nerve, just as if I had thousands of dollars behind my game. Finally the game took a turn, and in about an hour I was winner to the amount of three hundred and ninety dollars. Then I was very anxious to cease playing while I could redeem the checks and not expose myself, not knowing at what moment the run of luck would once more go against me. But it was early —I could invent no excuse to offer—so I kept on dealing until an incident occurred which put a summary stop to the proceedings, and released me from a very embarrassing position. A drunken man, passing along in front of the hotel, stumbled and fell through the window into the basement where we were playing, carrying sash and all with him in his sudden descent. Of course it produced a great confusion, and the cry of "Police!" being raised, the boys rushed from the table, removing a large scantling which had been placed against the door as a barrier, and making their escape in double quick time. I picked up money and kit and went to the office of the hotel, where I redeemed all my checks, and retired, about four hundred dollars ahead. Among those who played against me that night were a noted Chicago sport known as "Little Casino," and a notorious Toledo character, Joe Bean, who had just won a prize fight at Cheyenne, and who, I believe, would have murdered me if he had known that he had played in all of his pugilistic winnings against my three dollars. Dealing without capital, as I did that night, is grossly unprofessional, and no genuine sport would ever do it. I was "green" at the time, and had not learned my trade, or I would never have taken such a risk.

With these winnings in my pocket, I followed a trail to a room in the upper story of the hotel, where I was "braced" out of two hundred and fifty dollars. A "brace" game is, I may explain, one in which a man has no chance to win a bet unless the dealer breaks his finger, and that he never does.

For several years I never failed to attend all the trotting meetings on the Indiana and Michigan circuits. Many times I visited the races at Jackson, where I alternately lost and won large sums at faro, but invariably came out behind on the horses.

One day in 1872, when I was on the Jackson fair grounds, suffering from the effects of whisky and heat, I sustained a sunstroke, which laid me senseless on the ground. I was carried from the Park to the Union Hotel, where I remained unconscious for several days. I was then removed to Fort Wayne, and it was some time before I recovered from the attack, which came very near cutting me off in the midst of my wicked career.

The most memorable tour of the races I ever made was in 1876. This I shall always recollect as my "Centennial tour," and, as it was indeed full of incidents and adventures, and abounded in the ups and downs which characterize a gambler's life, I shall relate it somewhat in detail, as a fair specimen of my general experience in "following the trotters."

I began my summer trip at Peru, Indiana, where I opened a faro bank with a "roll" of eight hundred dollars, which disappeared in forty-eight hours. Meeting a Fort Wayne acquaintance, I borrowed twenty dollars, with which I visited a faro bank, played one deal, and drew out one hundred and twenty-five dollars. Hitherto I had usually bought the favorite in the pools, but had resolved to change my tactics this season, and buy the fields on all races, believing that was a sure way to win. I went to the Peru fair-grounds and invested my one hundred and twenty-five dollars in field pools on a trotting race, against Monarch, Jr., getting odds of five to one. I was cautioned by friends not to be so reckless, as they said Monarch, Jr., was sure to win. But I adhered to my programme, and the favorite was almost distanced in the first heat. The field won, and after the race I drew six hundred and twenty-five dollars from the pool-box, less the auctioneer's percentage. A friend of mine, a lumber dealer, who had lost four hundred dollars on Monarch, Jr., reproached me for not letting him into my "sure thing," and scarcely believed me when I told him I had bought blindly. This was the first race that I had beaten in three years, and the surprise was a great one.

I returned to Fort Wayne, where I remained over Sunday, and putting my room in charge of a couple of sports, told them I was off for a several months' tour. I then went to Jackson, where I lost every dollar I had, on faro the first morning, before breakfast. I laid idle at Jackson the remainder of the week, and when I left, my valise, well filled with clothing, remained at the hotel as security for the board bill. I worked my way to Saginaw as groom on the horse train, walked over to East Saginaw in the rain, and proceeded to the hotel. In the meantime I had borrowed one dollar, and purchased a ninety-nine cent pasteboard valise, upon the strength of which I expected to secure admission to the hotel. In this, however, I was sadly disappointed; as I entered the hotel, and approached the desk, the landlord cast a glance at me, let his eyes rest for a second upon my baggage, threw up his hands, and ejaculated: "We're all full." This cool reception was a decided surprise to me, but when I gazed upon my pasteboard satchel, it was easily explained; it had been melted down by the rain, and the sole contents — one pair of badly soiled hose — were plainly exposed to view. The situation was an awkward one, and without a word I hurried away, leaving my valise behind, amidst roars of laughter from the crowd who filled the office.

I succeeded in obtaining quarters at another hotel, raised a small stake, and in a short time had won five hundred and fifty dollars at faro. From Saginaw I went to Detroit, thence to Toledo, and next to Cleveland, where I witnessed the great race between Goldsmith Maid and Smuggler, which was won by the latter. It is said Budd Doble lost twenty-five thousand dollars on that match; it is therefore not strange that Mrs. Doble fainted in the private box of the amphitheater, when Smuggler passed under the wire leading the brave little mare.

The next place I visited was Buffalo. Since leaving home I had made several winnings, but upon departing from Buffalo my cash capital had diminished to six dollars. In company with an old friend, Joe Hull, of Toledo, I went to Niagara Falls to spend the Sabbath. We registered at the Cataract House, and proceeded to visit Goat Island and the other points of interest. This exhausted our funds, and we returned to the hotel in a penniless condition. I had obtained my valise from Jackson, and by means of a clever stratagem, we got it out of the Cataract House, and boarded the train for Rochester. Hull obtained passage by means of his remarkable cheek, while I was carried on the strength of a letter " To all Passenger Conductors," indorsing me as an old railroad man. This letter was written for me by a notorious safe-blower, and by its aid I traveled hundreds of miles on Eastern railroads. I never learned the price of board per day at the Cataract House.

Arriving at Rochester, I borrowed five dollars, which was promptly invested in cocktails. While in that city I was "staked," and made a winning of three hundred and twenty-five dollars on faro. I went on a terrible spree — during which time my money was taken from me for safe keeping — and left for Utica, but was so "tired" that I could not be awakened at that point, and was therefore carried through to Albany. Arriving at the latter place I found myself in my stocking feet, without funds, my valise gone, and one shoe in one car and one in another, with an empty whisky bottle in each. With much difficulty I gathered myself together, left the train, and entered the eating-house, where I got into conversation with a pleasant old gentleman, who talked to me kindly, and gave me some seasonable warnings against gamblers and three-card-monte men. I wondered how they could take any advantage of me in my impecunious condition, and hastily ate my breakfast, and in passing from the hall was accosted by a clerk, who demanded a dollar for the meal; pointing to the old gentleman, I said, "Father will settle that," and hurried away. I have often wondered how "dad" got out.

I went back to Utica, and remained there several days; soon after my arrival I got drunk, and my prolonged dissipation and exposure led to an attack of illness, which, though brief, was very severe.

During my stay in Utica I was so "light," financially, that I was unable most of the time to attend the races.

The city was crowded with people, and there was much gambling and robbing going on. The confidence men and monte players were in clover and counted their gains by the thousands. Among them was the most notorious and successful thief who ever operated in this country, "Canada Bill," whose name is familiar to every newspaper reader. He had rented for the week, at an exorbitant figure, a saloon on one of the principal streets of the city. Here he made his headquarters, and he had scores of "ropers" and "decoy ducks" on the streets, in the saloons, at the track, and, in fact, every where capturing "suckers." To these "cappers" he paid fifty per cent. of the amount realized from the "bloaks" they brought in. At the rear of the saloon there was a little room, carefully guarded, in which the robberies were committed. Only one party was allowed in this place at one time, so that the game might not be exposed to prospective dupes.

On the afternoon of the great races at Utica, a well-known Fort Wayne sport, whom I will call "Dan," and myself, found ourselves without sufficient means to attend. Our cash was limited to a small supply of "shinnies," and we concluded to pass away the time in playing dominoes for the beer. While thus engaged, an elderly, well-dressed, intelligent looking gentleman entered the saloon and called for a glass of beer. He watched us play for a moment, and asked us to join him in his refreshments, which, it is needless to say, we promptly did. We drank two or three times together, and, getting into conversation, we learned that the stranger was a leading attorney from Albany, who was in Utica trying an important canal case. The old gentleman, being somewhat overcome with the heat, stepped into a barber-shop near by and asked permission to sit in one of the chairs and cool himself off until the arrival of a customer. He sat down and soon fell asleep. I suggested to "Dan" that if we took him to Canada Bill's place, he might drop some money, and we would thus make a raise. "Dan" scouted the idea, saying he was too smart a man to be caught on three-card monte. But I thought not, and we determined at all events to make the effort. How to get the old gentleman out of the barber's chair was the first problem that presented itself. Just then I saw a poor demoralized looking tramp wandering aimlessly about, and as he evidently needed a dose of the razor, I handed him money enough to get shaved, instructing him to go into the barber shop and demand the chair occupied by our Albany

5*

friend. He did so, and the lawyer stepped out of the shop. Meeting us, he suggested another glass of beer, whereupon I remarked that the best beer I had found in Utica was at a saloon in the next block, and asked if we should not go there. All were agreed, and we proceeded to " Canada Bill's." While en route there the attorney spoke of the large number of confidence men in the city, and the rich harvest they were reaping. " Dan " and myself exchanged significant glances. This rather discouraged us, but we continued on our way. Arrived at Bill's establishment, we stepped into the back room, and I motioned for " Dutch Charley," of Chicago, the principal " capper," to come in and work the case, as I didn't understand it. We sat down at the table and were enjoying a glass of beer, when a rustic looking creature entered the room, munching a huge piece of pie, which he ate with palpable relish. He was a large man, dressed in coarse clothes, with a sunburnt countenance, a nose highly illuminated by the joint action of whisky and heat, and an expression of indescribable greenness and " freshness " about him. He at first seemed to notice no one, but sat down quietly at our table, and devoted himself strictly to his pie, until it had disappeared into his capacious stomach.

This strange looking creature naturally at-

THE DEMORALIZED TRAMP.

tracted our attention. The Albany man was particularly startled by the apparition, and after a careful survey of the new comer, ejaculated, "My God, see what we're coming to."

"Yes," responded I, "and we haven't got far to go unless we stop drinking."

The subject of our remarks, who seemed to be in blissful ignorance of the fact that we were discussing him, at this juncture, looked at us and said: "Gentlemen, wont ye'z huv a drink of suthin' with me?" We all declined the invitation, but continued to study the appearance and actions of the supposed "Hoosier," with much interest and amusement. He took no offense at our refusal, but quietly produced from the recesses of his great-coat pocket, a large roll of money, with a five hundred dollar bill for a wrapper. He noticed that we were watching him closely, and said:

"I done better with this 'ere druv of cattle than I done on t'other trip. This time I cleared five thousand dollars from my druv, but last time afore this them New York chaps skinned me, confound 'em." After a pause he continued: "But I had a little streak o' bad luck comin' down on the train from New York this mornin'. I met some strangers, and we had a little game with tickets like, and they bet me I couldn't turn the ticket, and won thirty-five dollars from me, durn their buttons."

"Why, man, you've been playing three-card monte," said our legal friend. "Don't you know better than that?"

"Thar, thar, that's what they called it; three-card monte, that's it. Wal, if they did get my thirty-five dollars, I took their tickets away from 'em, plague on 'em. I am goin' to larn that 'ere game myself, so I kin git my thirty-five dollars back."

With this remark, Canada Bill (for it was he) produced the cards, or tickets, as he called them, and began throwing them on the table in a very awkward manner. His clumsiness amused the party, and finally he said, "Wal, I want to get even, and I'll bet any man ten dollars he can't turn that 'ere ticket."

"Dutch Charley" was on hand, and promptly took the bet. After winning he said, "I'll bet you twenty, now."

"O, you're too lucky," said Bill, "I won't throw 'em agin for you, no how; but I'll try *you* for twenty dollars," continued he, turning to me, "and see how your luck is."

Charley slipped me a twenty dollar bill, and I won the bet. I offered to bet again, but Bill said:

"Thar, thar, I lost again. Wal, did you ever see sich luck. I'm out now nearly one hundred dollars on these durned tickets. I won't bet yer twenty dollars, but I'll just put up five hundred dollars agin any ov ye'z."

With this he turned the cards to win, the old gent from Albany meanwhile watching every movement closely, and evidently wholly engrossed in Bill's words and actions.

"I have only eight dollars, or I'd bet you," remarked he.

"Wal," said Bill, "I'll go yer two hundred dollars agin yer watch and chain."

"How do you know my watch and chain are worth two hundred dollars?"

"Wal, I didn't allow that a man o' yer standing wud war one that cost much less; of course I'd have to luk at it afore I'd bet that much agin it."

"It didn't cost me that much," said the gentleman, as Bill examined it.

"I couldn't go yez no more'n one hundred and ninety dollars, stranger, on that 'ere watch and chain."

The cards in the mean time had been lying on the table, and the attorney's eyes had never been removed from them. The bet was taken. Bill put his one hundred and ninety dollars in my hands, and the lawyer covered it with the watch, retaining the chain about his neck. In his excitement and haste to make the winning, which he considered a certainty, he reached to turn the card, when Bill covered the "tickets" with his hands, remarking: "Stranger, yer stake isn't all up yet."

Thereupon the gentleman removed the chain from his neck, handed it to me and then turned a card. Of course he lost, and as quick as a flash of lightning, a complete understanding of the situation dawned upon his mind. He leaned back in his chair, rubbed his eyes, took a careful survey of the gang by which he was surrounded, and propounded the following conundrum:

"Is it possible that I've been beat at three-card monte at last!"

"Yes, you've got beat," quickly answered the shark as I handed him the watch.

"Well boys," said the victim, who cared little for the pecuniary loss, but seemed humiliated at the fact that he had swallowed the bait, "I don't want to part with that watch and chain, because it was a present to me; how much will you take for it?"

"I've taken more than half a bushel of watches this week, and I don't know what to do with them, so I'll return this to you for one hundred dollars," said Bill, as quietly as if he were discussing the most legitimate business transaction.

"I don't think my fun has been worth over fifty dollars to me," responded the attorney, "but I will give you that amount."

HOW HE WAS "ROPED IN."

"Well, I'll take it, as I didn't have a great deal of trouble with you."

A check was produced, the attorney filled it out for fifty dollars, signed it, and recovered his watch and chain. Bill sent a messenger with him to a business house to get the money. Arriving at the door of the establishment, the gentleman said he was well known there and desired to enter alone to avoid any suspicion. He asked his companion for the check, saying he would go in, get it cashed, and bring out the money. The fellow handed the check over, the lawyer hastily tore it into fragments and dismissed the young man with a kind message to his master. Upon reporting the facts he found himself out of a situation. "Bill," after all, lost his swag, and "Dan" and I failed to get our percentage. This was my first and last experience as "capper" for a confidence man. Canada Bill made many thousands of dollars that year during the races. He was a most expert operator and among his victims were many persons of intelligence and experience. The only way to avoid such sharks is not to bet on any thing, and I have described this game in detail, for the purpose of exposing the *modus operandi* of the sharpers who go about in search of victims, thus placing my readers upon their guard. "Bill" squandered his money very lavishly and drank himself to death in about a year after the incident I have related. He died a pauper.

From Utica I went to Saratóga where I remained about ten days, during which I witnessed the great steeple-chase race which caused so much excitement and upon which half a million dollars is said to have changed hands. Vast sums were invested upon Osage. This horse was in the lead and had cleared nine of the twelve hurdles, when he fell and broke his neck, killing his rider at the same time. It was generally believed that the accident was caused by an attempt to pull him. After this my financial condition was such that I was compelled to walk to town. Repairing to the Grand Union Hotel where I had been sojourning, I explained my position to the clerk.

"I bet on Osage," said I.

"So did I," said the clerk.

"But I'm busted and a thousand miles from home," said I.

"Well, among twenty-five hundred guests we can afford to have one gentleman," said he as he marked my bill paid.

"When do you leave," continued he.

"When do you want me to leave?" asked I.

"Just as soon as you conveniently can," was the polite answer, and I was one of the passengers on the next train for the West.

I traveled on the railroad letter before referred to. Only once did I have any difficulty with a conductor; that was between Syracuse and Buffalo. He looked at my letter and said, "all right, get off," when I rose to go, sorrowfully remarking:

"Is it possible that I have been a slave to railroad corporations all my life only to be treated this way at last!"

This touched the conductor's heart, and he carried me to Buffalo, where I arrived with eighty cents on hand.

I had then been absent from home fourteen weeks, which had been passed in the most reckless dissipation. I had abused myself in every way, had deprived myself of food and sleep, and lived on whisky for days at a time. I now began to feel the inevitable effects of this course, and at Cleveland I found myself suffering from *delirium*, the horrors of which no pen can adequately portray. I imagined myself pursued by a vast drove of cattle, which swarmed about me, and followed me wherever I went; they were continually on my trail, and by no efforts of the will, could I avoid the dread apparition. I crossed the street, only to find them there before me; I turned a corner, only to see them coming toward me. I treaded on my tip toes, trying to steal away from them, but it was useless; I fully realized my terrible condition, and, fearing that I was about to die,

I took the train for home. When I entered the cars, the herd of steers went in the door with me; when I looked out the window, there they were, keeping pace with the train, and increased an hundred fold; waking or sleeping, they were ever before me. When I reached Fort Wayne, I thought to avoid them by hurriedly leaving the train, and going stealthily and quietly to my room, but I had taken only a few steps, when the entire herd, that had followed me from Cleveland, seemed to have concentrated into one huge ox, with piercing eyes and swelling nostrils, and a great horn in front. This prodigious animal, which stood ever in my path, seemed coming toward me, and I stepped into the gutter to avoid him. There he was also, and, in my despair, I reached forth to seize him by the horn, but he eluded my grasp. I passed several nights, which were filled with the most fearful horrors, at my room. So ungovernable was I in my terrible suffering, that I could induce no one to sleep with me through an entire night. Those dreadful cattle were still with me; waking or sleeping, they were ever before my eyes. In the vain hope of relief, I left the city, and went to Waterloo, where I remained several days and nights, undergoing the most severe physical and mental torment. In my room was a nail head protruding from the wall, which, when I reclined

AN ATTACK OF DELIRIUM.

upon the bed, appeared, to my distorted vision, in all kinds of grotesque and horrid shapes. It assumed the outline of a wild animal, seeming about to plunge at me, and tear me to pieces, then it resumed its natural form, and seemed to swell to the size of half a bushel; and, anon, it took some other strange and forbidding aspect. I left my bed, perhaps, a score of times that night to feel of this nail head, in the endeavor to convince myself that it was not what it seemed to be; but it was useless.

Very slowly I recovered from the effects of my terrible debauch, and from my severe and prolonged attack of *delirium tremens*, which had well-nigh proved fatal. Strange to say, the fearful warning I received had but little effect upon me. For a time, I was comparatively temperate, but before long I was again indulging the degraded appetite, which had so long held me in its power.

In 1877, I visited the races, at Grand Rapids, Jackson, Detroit, Cleveland, and other points. I reached Detroit in company with a seedy looking gang of sports, and we all registered at the Gaffnet House; I was then in funds, and paid five dollars, in advance, for board. The most of my companions, however, were penniless, and the landlord, whose name the hotel bore, took one look at them, went up stairs, and died. It was said that he died of apoplexy, but I always imagined that the shabby appearance of his new guests was the main cause of his sudden taking off.

The races proved a failure on account of the restrictions placed upon gambling, and the sports failed to make a raise. Upon the day of Mr. Gaffnet's funeral they followed his remains out of the hotel, valises in hand, being the principal mourners, and taking the first boat, hastily crossed into Canada. I also went into Her Majesty's dominions, and passed a few days with a congenial party, at a small place called Brandenburg, where we indulged freely in white wheat whisky. I then proceeded to Cleveland, and feeling the premonitory symptoms of *delirium*, I sobered up, and swore a solemn oath to drink no more. But, notwithstanding this vow, in less than twenty-four hours after my arrival in Cleveland, I was beastly drunk. I made a winning of one hundred and twenty-five dollars, and remained there two weeks, waiting for the races, during which time I drank freely. When I arrived home, in August, 1877, I was exhausted, penniless, discouraged, and again on the verge of *delirium tremens*. That was my last experience in "following the trotters."

CHAPTER VII.

THE VARIOUS PHASES OF GAMBLING—GOOD AND BAD QUALITIES OF THE GENUINE SPORTING MAN—PREVALENCE OF THE VICE AMONG BUSINESS MEN—THE MISERY AND RUIN IT CAUSES—A FEW WORDS TO THE SPORTING FRATERNITY.

My fifteen years experience as a gambler gave me, I think, a pretty thorough knowledge of sporting men, and a clear insight into their characters, habits, and modes of life. The world at large really knows very little about the men who gain a livelihood by "bucking the tiger," and a few words concerning them will not, I fancy, prove either uninteresting or superfluous.

Gambling is, I have somewhere said, a trade which can only be mastered by careful study, long practice, and keen observation. In this, as in everything else, experience is the best, if at the same time the dearest, teacher. The young gambler finds no one to instruct him in the mysteries of the calling which he has chosen. He learns his lessons one by one, as I learned mine, at the cost of many severe losses; and however long he may follow the seductive but evil pursuit which he has embraced, he will never be able to truthfully say that he understands it thoroughly.

Let me present, for the entertainment of the reader, a picture of the typical gambler. He finds, upon entering the fraternity, that it has its own code of morals, to which he must adhere rigorously, if he would enjoy the respect and confidence of the members. Sporting men are, in a certain sense, detached from the outside world. They follow a vocation which the public very properly holds to be immoral, and which the laws of all civilized States forbid, but which, by its professors, is believed to be entirely legitimate and honorable. They demand of each other a strict adherence to a certain standard, which, however false and pernicious it may be, is by them regarded as an infallible test of manhood and decency. A gambler, to be successful, and well regarded by his associates, must be possessed of iron nerve; must accept the successes and reverses of fortune with equal imperturbability; must be generous and extravagant to an excessive degree; and must, above all, keep his word beyond suspicion. These requirements are imperative, and the so-called gambler who fails to comply with them is without standing or influence among his fellows. A miser, a liar, and a man without nerve and grit, who "kicks" at every reverse of fortune, is but poorly regarded among sporting men, and is treated by them with the utmost coldness and indifference.

There are perhaps other essentials in the character of a successful and popular gambler, but the ones I have named are the most important. This will be the testimony of every man who knows any thing whatever of the subject.

The gambler who has no nerve is a pronounced failure from the beginning. He will never accomplish any thing, and might as well recognize it from the start. The experienced sporting man will sit down at the table and win or lose thousands of dollars without changing expression or uttering a single exclamation. The very heaviest games — those in which large fortunes are risked upon the turn of a card, and in which men are enriched or beggared in a single evening — are conducted with the utmost decorum and amidst the most profound silence. A man enters the room, seats himself at a table, and mayhap places all his worldly wealth upon a card. The turn is made; he loses, and withdraws from the game as quietly, and apparently as unconcerned, as if he had been but a disinterested spectator.

Again, he lays down an insignificant sum, and rises in a short time the possessor of thousands; his demeanor is as impassive, his countenance as imperturbable, as before. The gambler, however deeply he may feel his loss, or however much elated he may be with his winning, must not in any way give vent to his emotions in a gaming room, or he will speedily lose caste and be pronounced a "dogan."

This so-called nerve leads to a certain recklessness or foolhardiness, which always characterizes a genuine sporting man. I have already illustrated this quality by several marked instances, among them that of the men who played with such coolness and passiveness while on the skirmish line, with bullets whistling past their ears, and occasionally killing or wounding a comrade; and also that of the indomitable players who, with an adjoining building in flames, and terrific explosions taking place in their immediate vicinity, sat at the faro table with as much calmness as they would eat their dinner. Of course such instances are, in a large degree, to be attributed to the terrible fascination which gaming has for its votaries, of the strength of which no one who has not fallen within its power can form the most feeble conception; but it is also particularly to be ascribed to the quality of nerve which is so characteristic of a genuine sport, and which his avocation naturally inspires.

The recklessness which makes a gambler "lose his pile" without whimpering, or coolly "buck the tiger" in a burning building, also makes him improvident, careless of the future, and lavishly extravagant with his money, when he has any. There is no class of men in the world who spend money so freely and so foolishly as sporting men. They stop at the most expensive hotels; travel in the most princely style; wear the finest clothing and most valuable jewelry; drive the fastest horses; smoke the most costly cigars, and drink the rarest of wines. There is no luxury which a gambler will not enjoy if he has, or can get, the money to pay for it. He will spend his last dollar for a superfluous article as freely and thoughtlessly as if he had a million of them in bank; and his motto seems to be, "Eat, drink, and be merry, for to-morrow ye die."

The gambler becomes a spendthrift, not only from inclination, but also because of the habits of those with whom he associates, and because they demand that he should be. It matters not how saving or frugal he may naturally be, he must squander his money recklessly, or his reputation will fall below par. Therefore, in order to get the name, he will spend his money in a silly way and in the most ostentatious manner, however hard it may be for him to do.

In order to maintain his reputation, the average sport will do many extremely silly things. I remember pawning my overcoat in the dead of winter for less than one-third of its value, and out of the proceeds paying one dollar and fifty cents for a dinner, and topping off with a twenty-five cent cigar. The sport thinks nothing of spending several dollars over a bar "treating" a crowd, in order to "keep up his 'rep.'" when he has to step out shortly afterward and borrow a few cents with which to buy a beefsteak for his family—that is, if they get any, which is very doubtful.

In cities where there is much gambling and many sports, retail trade is always brisk, in many departments. The gamesters scatter their money lavishly about, and their patronage puts thousands of dollars into the pockets of tradesmen. Among the institutions which invariably flourish where gamblers abound, are saloons and pawnbroker shops. Of course they are liberal patrons of the former, and a very large proportion of their winnings finds its way over the bar. Of the pawnbroker's shops, they are regular customers, and in them they are fleeced most unmercifully. They rarely obtain one-third the value of the article which they pledge. In a majority of instances, they are unable to redeem them at the specified time, and thus for a small sum, they lose a watch or a diamond which cost them a handsome amount. Even if they make redemption, they have to pay from one hundred to one hundred and twenty per cent. interest, and in either case they are thoroughly "done for."

A large majority of sporting men, although apparently callous and hardened, are, in truth, kind hearted and charitable to a remarkable degree. They rarely refuse to extend relief in a case of distress, if they have any means, and I have seen many sports give up their last dollar to help some poor unfortunate person out of difficulty. They are also liberal donors to benevolent and charitable institutions. I myself, when in the midst of my depraved career, have given goodly sums to churches which I never expected to enter, and a great many of my associates did likewise. I do not ascribe these acts altogether to goodness of heart. They are performed from a variety of motives. The gambler, being careless of money, is apt to give it away as freely as he would expend it for some superfluous article. He frequently contributes to benevolent objects in order to gain friends and acquaintances among business men, some of whom he hopes may visit his establishment. These investments, may, he hopes, tend to remove the prejudice existing against him and his calling, and save him from prosecution. Sometimes I think these acts are performed as a kind of conscience offering, and that the sporting man believes such deeds may atone in some way for his wicked life.

There is a certain code of honor—so-called—which prevails among the gambling fraternity, and to which every member must adhere, under penalty of losing his popularity and standing. This code is based upon a false standard, and I couldn't recommend it to society or the world at large, but such as it is, it is strictly observed by every man who is recognized as a genuine sport. It requires the most rigid adherence to one's word in every instance. All a gambler has to rely upon is his word, and when he becomes known as a liar or a betrayer of confidence, he is regarded, not as a gambler, but as a common thief. Wherever he may go, he will find that his reputation has preceded him. He is a "marked man" and will obtain no recognition or confidence at the hands of professionals. I can truthfully say, after all my experience among this class of people, that I would as readily take the word of a regular sporting man on a business transaction as that of any person in the community. I know men in this business who stand so well that they receive a salary of twenty to forty dollars per day, and are trusted with the possession of many thousands of dollars.

The gambler looks upon his occupation as perfectly legitimate, and believes it is conducted as honorably as are most branches of business which the law recognizes. There is some truth in this theory. I believe there is as much gambling done in our boards of trade and produce exchanges as at faro banks and poker rooms, and I fail to see the distinction between betting on the price of corn or on the turn of a card. That one is wrong, does not, however, excuse the other. I believe that neither is right, and that Christian people should condemn them both.

Gamblers regard it as perfectly legitimate to take advantage of each other at play in any possible way, unless it involves a betrayal of confidence. This is held to be a part of the trade, and the sports believe that no man has any business to play unless he has mastered his trade. This is the work of a lifetime, and the veterans in the craft not infrequently find themselves beaten by schemes and devices which are intended for amateurs. This being the case, it can readily be seen that the business man, or the occasional player, has a poor chance to win in the majority of games. If I were to advise this class of men to play at all, I would say: Enter some game with the most thorough and skillful gamblers—men who know enough to protect themselves—and the chances are that the game will be on the square, and that you will stand an even chance of winning, if you use the necessary amount of judgment. There are plenty of such games played, but the difficulty for amateurs is to know where they are to be found.

I have, I think, done full justice to the character of the true sporting man. I have given due weight to the good qualities by which he is usually characterized, and which are not properly appreciated by the world at large. The reason for this is, that there are many men who claim to be sports when they have no right to the appellation.

The public classes gamblers in the same category as thieves and murderers, principally because so many of the riff-raff and scum of humanity advertise themselves as sporting men. They do this mainly in order to shield themselves from the penalties of the law, which would otherwise be visited upon them; and by their actions they compel gamblers to bear a greater weight of odium than is their due. These fellows, in many instances, have started out as gamblers, but by reason of their dishonesty, falsehood, and betrayals of confidence, have been dropped from the ranks, and become ordinary thieves and loafers. They hang around gambling rooms as much as possible, and are always ready to do any thing low or mean. They rarely have money enough to sit in a gambler's game, and when they do are easily beaten. They give their word when they know they can not keep it good; they "rope in" business men and strangers, and for a small sum profess to give them "points," which frequently makes them suspicious, and drives them from the room. They finally become "crabbers," that is, men who steal a stake from the table when the owner's back is turned, and who would not hesitate to pick a pocket, or to commit any crime whatever. These fellows claim to be gamblers, and are so classed by the press and the public, and the genuine sports are held responsible for their shortcomings. Truth compels me to say that there are a hundred of this class of men in the country where there are ten true sports; that the proportion is increasing every year, and that the business of gambling is becoming more and more degraded, and rapidly being shorn of its few redeeming features. These thieves are ruining the sport at horse races, as well as at the gaming rooms, and through their conduct the sporting profession is becoming more disreputable than ever.

Probably few of my readers have any idea how many business men are addicted to gambling. The heads of large mercantile houses, the jobber, the merchant, the importer, and the banker, as well as the small tradesman, and the employé, are frequently to be found sitting around the gaming table. Gamblers use their utmost efforts to secure visits from this class of men; for sports realize that they can not earn a living from each other, but that they must draw from producers, and those who amass money by legitimate means. It is scarcely necessary to say that, with hardly an exception, the business man gets the worst of it, in "bucking the tiger." I can truthfully say that in all my experience, I never have known one of this class who was not worse off, by reason of playing, while I have known scores of them to be ruined financially, morally, and physically, by an indulgence of their gambling propensities. It is obvious that such should be the case. When men who devote their whole time and attention to sporting, can not master its details, how can the man do so who plays in his leisure hours for amusement? It is singular to me that men of fine business capacity, sound judgment, good common sense, high social standing, and frequently, I regret to say, of religious professions, will allow themselves to be so deeply fascinated by the allurements of the card table, that they will sacrifice time, money, health, position, character, everything, to its never-ceasing demands.

I can look back to the year 1865, and recall many men who were then in prosperous circumstances, doing a lucrative business, occupying a fine social position, who have since gone to their ruin, by reason of gambling. Many once happy and comfortable families have been reduced to want and beggary, because he who should have made provision for them, has sacrificed their future welfare, as well as his own position and prospects, to his insane and senseless passion for the card table.

The business man who seeks the gaming room for recreation, often falls into the hands of the class of thieves to whom I have referred, and who undertake to post him for a "consideration." After a course of instruction the amateur imagines that he knows all the mysteries of faro and poker; but a few heavy losings convince him to the contrary. He attempts to recover what he has sacrificed, and in so doing he loses what he has left. He is speedily reduced from affluence to poverty, and from poverty to absolute want and beggary. In the meantime, he has neglected his business, lost his trade, allowed his notes to be protested, his creditors have closed him up, his name figures in the bankruptcy lists, and his friends ascribe his failure to "hard times" and "scarcity of money." Reduced to this point, he hovers around the place which has proved his ruin, and vainly endeavors to retrieve his fortune, where he has wasted it. His late hours, evil associates, and reverses, lead him to drinking. He descends the ladder, step by step, loses the friends of former years, becomes an outcast, and a vagrant, and finally dies a drunkard, and fills a pauper's grave.

This is no fancy sketch; I have known many such cases as the above, and they are more numerous than the public imagines. I believe more business failures result from gambling, than from any other one cause, and I hold that the business man who plays, expecting to win in the long run, is an idiot who should be sent to an asylum. The experiences of those who have trod this path, and observation of the sad examples all about him, arising from play, not to speak of the dictates of good common sense, should teach him that gambling can result in nothing but loss and disappointment and ultimately, if persisted in, complete and irretrievable ruin.

But if it is folly for a business or professional man to gamble, it is equally so for any person to adopt sporting as a means of gaining a livelihood. The life of a gambler is a hard one. I know it has a kind of fascination for thoughtless and reckless young men who desire to live without work, to enjoy a career of "pleasure," and to "see the world," but they will find in due time that there is no genuine pleasure connected with a sporting life.

The gambler is really a hard worker. He lives in defiance, not only of human, but also of divine laws. He violates, in his daily life, the precepts of nature, which all mankind should follow. He reverses the established order and turns his nights into days, and his days into nights. When more favored men are passing the evenings at their happy homes with their wives and little ones, or in social pleasures or literary pursuits, the gambler sits in his heated room, under the blazing gas jet, breathing a foul and polluted atmosphere, hearing occasionally a ribald jest or a blasphemous expression, his nerves strained to their utmost tension, despite the unchanging expression of his countenance, and his whole nature, moral, mental, and physical, tainted by his evil surroundings. And after the world has gone to rest, and tired humanity is seeking "nature's sweet restorer, sleep," the gambler is still at his table, dealing his cards with the steady monotony of a machine, his head throbbing, his eyelids heavy, his body feverish, his strength exhausted. And at last, when the first streaks of dawn are seen upon the eastern horizon, and the pale, dim light of early morning heralds the approach of day, he goes to his couch and seeks rest at a time when all about him are awakening from their slumbers. Call you this pleasure? I call it hardship and misery. I solemnly affirm that in all the years of my sporting life, I never enjoyed one moment of real, genuine happiness. I would not exchange one hour of my existence since my conversion, for all the years of my sinful life.

The gambler varies the monotony of his life

with riotous excesses and extravagant indulgence. His amusements, like his business, are degrading morally and injurious physically. His varying fortunes render his life a feverish and unsatisfactory one. He is ostracized from society, debarred from the enjoyments of domestic pleasures, and incapacitated for literary entertainment. He wears out his existence in a few years, undermines his constitution by exposure and dissipation, is shabbily treated by the goddess of fortune whom he has wooed so long, and dies a pauper in the prime of life. But one gambler in a hundred lives to old age; and not one in a hundred dies the possessor of any property. The career which to many looks so inviting, ends at last in shame and penury, and the "man of pleasure," falsely so called, is only a creature of misery and sorrow.

Where are the gamblers who flourished ten or twelve years ago, during the flush times? I can recall the names of many who, since that time, have gone over the precipice, dying in beggary, without a thought or hope for the future. Kind-hearted, genial, whole-souled Tim McCarthy, the champion billiardist of Indiana, won thousands of dollars at his keno bank, and other games, and squandered it all in dissipation, and after a few years of reckless drinking, stood up before a mirror in a Chicago saloon, and in a fit of despair blew out his brains. Billy Grunauer, ten years ago, was the leading sporting man of Northern Indiana. He dressed in the extreme of fashion, wore the costliest clothing, and the rarest diamonds, smoked imported cigars, drank the most expensive wines, and drove a thousand dollar team. But this could not last, and poor Billy was borne to his grave a few months ago from the St. Joseph's hospital, where he had been suffering from a hopeless disease for months.

For several years before his death he had been a sorrowful object in our midst; broken in health, downcast in spirits, and without a penny out of all the thousands he had won at gaming, he saw his end rapidly approaching without any care for his future state, or any hope of happiness beyond the grave. The last time he was on the streets he took dinner with me, and I asked him "if he ever thought of his eternal state?"

"Yes," said he, "I guess they will come three-a-side over there; I have tried it here a long time, but it won't work."

He referred, in this expression, to his favorite system of playing the bank. In a few days he died, and but for the kindness of relatives his burial would have been that of a pauper.

I could name many other men who have been regarded as prosperous and successful gamblers, who died penniless and friendless. Captain Phillips, of Toledo, who played poker for thirty years, and whose winnings on the game aggregated a vast sum, died in Lima, Ohio, without enough to bury him. Joe Bean, of Toledo, the prize fighter and gambler, died in early manhood under similar circumstances, and I might enumerate such instances indefinitely. I have never known a sporting man to die rich, and the most of them have passed away without leaving enough assets to pay their funeral expenses. Even John Morrissey, who handled millions of dollars, and conducted the largest games in the world, died insolvent; and when he failed who can hope to succeed?

It does not pay to be a gambler. The life is a hard one, but the death is still harder. The years of the gambler are few, and they are not happy ones. I can conceive of no inducement for a man to enter this occupation. Sporting men are drones; what the world wants is workers. There are too many men who want to live without labor. Gaming no longer offers the attractions that it once did. There is less money in the country than there was ten years ago, but the ranks of the gamblers are overcrowded. The most of them can not make a living unless they steal, and hence it is that the fraternity is becoming more corrupt and degraded every year. The times have changed, and we must change with them. The man who seeks to live off the earnings of others is an enemy to society and must be treated as such. I earnestly advise every sporting man who reads these pages, to give up his nefarious business, pull up his sleeves and go to work as I have done. It is no disgrace to work; it is creditable and honorable. If they don't do so, the State will finally take steps to compel them; it is only a question of time. The large number of sporting men now in the country are a burden to society, which will and must be thrown off. I speak these words frankly and soberly, but in all kindness. I realize, as I never did before, the sinfulness of this vice, and the wrong which a man does himself, his fellow man, and his God by wasting his existence in its practice. I can see that its inevitable end is a miserable death, amidst poverty and despair, and a future of suffering and remorse. I shudder when I think of the fate I have so narrowly escaped. I would that my words could reach every sporting man in America, and that they could be led to comprehend the folly, wickedness, and unprofitableness of the careers they are leading.

CHAPTER VIII.

HOW I BECAME A CONVERT TO THE MURPHY CAUSE — SIGNING THE PLEDGE — STRUGGLES WITH THE DEMON ALCOHOL — FINAL TRIUMPH OVER THE RUM DEVIL.

In the latter part of July, 1877, I arrived home, after a tour of the races, in a deplorable condition. I had lost all of my money and was suffering from the effects of a prolonged spree. My personal debts amounted to at least fifteen hundred dollars, and I had no means of paying any portion of them. Upon my return I found my game had run down very badly, and the outlook was certainly a discouraging one. The "boys" failed to visit my room as was their wont, and when I inquired the reason, they replied, "O, we go to the Rink every evening; all the fun is over there now." I knew there was a temperance movement in progress in Fort Wayne, but had not realized what proportions it had assumed. Night after night my rooms were deserted and it was impossible to get up a game. Finally I concluded to attend one of the meetings, partly to gratify some of my old associates, but principally from curiosity. The Rink holds sixteen hundred people, and when I entered it, I found, greatly to my surprise, that it was crowded to its utmost capacity. I remained until the close of the meeting and in spite of myself was greatly interested in the proceedings. At the conclusion of the exercises I returned to my room in a thoughtful mood. I found a few "regulars" gathered there. I said, "It's no wonder that we have no game any more, every body is at the Rink. If this thing keeps on I don't know what will become of us." "Neither do I," spoke up a saloon keeper, who seemed greatly depressed at the outlook. "I am not doing one third of the business I did a year ago. If the Murphys don't stop pretty soon, I for one shall be ruined."

I thought seriously over the situation and finally came to the conclusion that perhaps the movement would help the gambling business. I reasoned that if men stopped drinking they would have more money to gamble with, although the experience I was having with my game did not sustain the argument. I failed then to realize that the two vices go together, and lead to one another; that the gambler is almost invariably a drinker, and the drinker very frequently a gambler. A man who is addicted to drinking is almost certain to get to playing, and he who gambles will, sooner or later, become a drunkard.

The next evening my room was again empty, and impelled by some power I did not comprehend, but could not resist, I again joined the crowd and wended my way to the "Old Ark" as the Rink was called. I found another large meeting in progress, although this was the fifth week of the series. The greatest enthusiasm prevailed, and almost everybody in the house looked cheerful and happy. The gentleman who conducted the meeting spoke in a very encouraging strain, of the results. "During the past week," he said, "twelve hundred persons have signed the pledge and donned the blue ribbon, making thirty-five hundred signers in all since we began our campaign." This opened my eyes still wider, and again I found myself inquiring, "What will the result be."

Every night my room was empty and my game closed, and I drifted into the meetings at the Rink. The movement was being conducted by Rusk and Reddick, two energetic young workers from Pittsburgh, and they had already been the agents, under God, of reclaiming many of the most dissipated men in the city from lives of intemperance and debauchery. My frequent attendance upon the meetings had attracted much attention, and my motives were generally discussed among the temperance people. One night Mr. Rusk addressed me, saying:

"I want you to sign the pledge." To say that I was amazed, but feebly describes my feelings—I was dumbfounded. I looked at him closely, for I had a curiosity to see any man who had the effrontery to ask me to sign a temperance pledge. I made fun of him, and remarked that if the government had sent me out after pirates I would have "tackled him the first man." He laughed, taking my abuse in the best of humor. Finally he asked my business.

"Business? Well, you just make your collection and go with me to my room, and if I can beat aces up for you—you'll know what my business is."

At this Mr. Rusk smiled, and said "I've been there, my boy. I've gambled and know all about it, as well as many other vices. If you don't give it up you'll find out in the long run that there is no money in it."

I laughed and continued to chaff him, when he left me, saying, "I'll see you again." He *did* see me again; every time I met him he chatted with me in a pleasant, good-natured way, and I soon learned to like him. Finally I invited him to my rooms, and he accepted. He found them gorgeously furnished, with handsome Brussels carpet, elegant sideboards, and all of the appurtenances of a first-class "gambling hell." Mr. Rusk did not play with me, but he evidently understood the business, and used his knowledge to good advantage in his argument with me. He asked me if I would not be a much more successful gambler if I did not drink, and if I had not lost hundreds, perhaps thousands, of dollars because of my fondness for liquor. Of course I had, and I frankly admitted it; I had just returned from a prolonged spree, having wasted large winnings in drink. I related a number of my experiences, and Mr. Rusk said his had been similar, although on a smaller scale. We both agreed that if I were to stop drinking I would prosper and make plenty of money.

It was evident that Mr. Rusk understood my case perfectly. He did not try to force me to sign the pledge against my will, but he continued to meet me every day and exchange a few words with me. He frequently referred to the mistakes of his past life, all of which had a personal application I could not fail to make. I told him "his life had been something like mine, but that I had drifted farther out into the current than he, and that it would be useless for me to sign the pledge, because it would be impossible for me to keep it." I added that "to take the pledge and then dishonor it would be ten times worse than never to sign it at all." He agreed with me in this, and said he could not respect a man who "signed for fun," not intending to keep his word; he was sure, however, I could take the pledge and keep it, and he urged me to come forward at the next meeting, take a bold stand, and don the blue ribbon; he had no doubt that I would honor the pledge if I signed it. Again I refused; I told him that I would not attempt an impossibility; I couldn't stop drinking, and wouldn't try. He left me, for the first time appearing discouraged. The next meeting, however, found me present, as usual. I went with a friend of mine, Mr. Charles Reed, a young man whom I respected for his good habits; although he never drank or gambled, he had joined the "Murphies," and urged me to do likewise. I told him as I told Mr. Rusk, that it was no use, I could not give up drink. That evening the signers came thick and fast, and the enthusiasm was unbounded. After the exercises were over, we remained while the noble workers solicited signatures, and urged the poor inebriates to emancipate themselves from their slavery. For some reason I couldn't leave, and soon I found myself surrounded by a bevy of ladies. This was evidently a piece of strategy on the part of Mr. Reed, for I noticed him standing at a distance, greatly amused at my predicament. The ladies made a combined assault upon me, and insisted upon my signing the pledge. I repeated to them what I had said to so many others, that I could not keep it; one of them said I must sign it if I had to stay all night; I told her that if I did as she asked I would certainly dishonor the pledge, and *that* I was determined not to do. Meanwhile the crowd about me was getting larger all the time, and I noticed I was becoming the cynosure of all eyes. My situation was novel and embarrassing, and I began to think of some method of escape. I had seen three years of hard service in the army, and had been through many battles, but this seemed to me the most trying engagement of my life. I had determined not to surrender, but to beat a masterly retreat, and inwardly resolved that if I ever got out of the Rink I would *never* enter it again until the meetings commenced. But the ladies had resolved to capture me for the Murphy army, and would not take "no" for an answer; they entreated me to embrace the good cause, and plied me with arguments which were well nigh irresistible. My position was becoming momentarily more desperate, and as a final resource, I said: "Ladies, let me go to-night, and I promise by all that is good and holy that I will come back to-morrow night and sign the pledge, and I will live up to it." But the ladies didn't believe me, and really they had no reason to; I had no intention of keeping my promise, my only idea being to get out of the Rink; my firm determination was never to attend another Murphy meeting. The ladies didn't want to take my promise, but a little lady who was in the group spoke up and said, in her childish way, "Let him go, Mamma, he is speaking the truth; he will come back to-morrow night and sign the pledge. You will, won't you?" added the little one, appealing to me. "Of course I will," said I, seeing at last a chance of escape. The girl's simple faith in my word outweighed the doubts of the ladies, and they opened a way for me to pass out. I left the Rink with a settled purpose never to visit it again while the meetings continued.

I hastened to my room, thinking over the incidents of the evening and congratulating myself upon my fortunate escape. Thoughts of the little girl who had rescued me, came to my mind. I asked myself, "Why did she believe me, when in fact I was telling a lie." I tried to forget the evening's experience, but I could not do so. I endeavored to divert my mind by a game of poker, but I was abstracted and careless, and in a few moments had lost forty dollars. I arose and walked restlessly about the room. The angel face of that child was ever before my eyes, and her words were constantly sounding in my ears:—"He is telling the truth, Mamma. You will come back, won't you, and sign the pledge?"

I put on my hat, left my room, and sought a

saloon, where I tried to solace myself with billiards. The attempt was a failure; I could not fix my attention on the game. I laid down my cue and walked out into the street; I could not by any artifice withdraw my thoughts from the one subject which burdened them, nor shut out the sound of the little lady's simple words. Slowly I walked toward my rooms, vainly struggling to compose my mind. When I arrived at the club room, the game was over and the room deserted. I entered my chamber, adjoining the gambling hall, and prepared for bed. I laid down, but sleep did not come to my eyelids. I tossed about feverishly, struggling to overcome my restlessness, but without result. I attempted to argue with myself, but the effort was in vain. I arose from my bed and tried to relieve the strain upon my mind by reading. It was of no avail. I read all the newspapers in the room, but did not comprehend one word in them. When I laid them down I did not remember any thing they contained. Again I sought my bed, but my mental unrest continued. I rolled about in my agony, but no peace came to me. The hours dragged wearily along, and one subject continued uppermost in my mind. I gave up the effort to banish it. Morning at last came, and I rejoiced over the termination of the longest night I had ever passed. But daylight brought no calm to my troubled brain. It was still in a chaotic state, and the same words were ever present: "You will come back to-morrow night and sign the pledge, won't you?"

I went to my hotel, but scarcely tasted breakfast. Then I wandered aimlessly about the streets, and found the day I had so longed for to be even more dismal than the dreary night whose minutes had seemed hours. My condition was, in brief, one of mental torture, and I felt as though if relief did not soon come, I should go crazy. That night I involuntarily sought the Rink, arriving there almost as soon as it was lighted up. I was among the first arrivals, and upon meeting Mr. Rusk, I told him I would sign the pledge at once if he would assure me that the newspapers would say nothing about it. The press had, for many years, devoted a great deal of attention to me, and I feared that, if the city journals should publish me as a Murphy convert, I would become a butt for the ridicule of all the sports and bummers in the city. I was among the first that evening to step forward and sign the pledge. As I affixed my name, the old building fairly shook with the cheers of sixteen hundred people. In a moment I was surrounded by a host of ladies and gentlemen who shook me warmly by the hand, and congratulated me eartily upon the step I had taken. Many spoke to me, who had never before exchanged a word with me, but who had always regarded me as the concentrated essence of wickedness.

As soon as I had signed the pledge I felt relieved. A great weight seemed to be lifted from my soul, and I left for my rooms after the meeting in a much happier frame of mind than on the preceding evening.

The only thing I dreaded was newspaper publicity. The journals of the city had devoted many columns to me in connection with gambling, horse racing, and arrests for various misdemeanors, and I disliked to have my name published in connection with any thing so good and holy as the temperance cause. But I called to mind Mr. Rusk's assurance on this score, and retired without any misgivings. The next morning, upon arising, I picked up the *Gazette* and discovered to my amazement a column report of my surrender to the Murphys. At this I was greatly disgusted, and I at once decided to go and get drunk. I left the room with that intention, but I soon began to think of the many good people who had taken me so warmly by the hand the night before, and bade me God speed. What would they think of me, should I thus deliberately and openly violate my solemn pledge? This was something strange for me, for I had never before cared for the opinion of the sober, and temperate, and religious community. I passed along the streets, and the first persons I met were saloon keepers. They refused to speak to me, and I admit that I felt the slight. But by this time I was settled in my purpose to stick to the pledge.

My old companions enjoyed themselves greatly at my expense, and they subjected me to all kinds of ridicule. Many bets were made upon the length of time I would abstain from drinking, the limits ranging from six hours to ten days. One saloon keeper predicted that I would hold out three weeks, and no longer. He said that he had gauged my stomach, and that at the end of three weeks on cold water diet I would be ripe for a big drunk. An attempt was made to sell pools on me, but no one would bet on my "sticking" more than three weeks. I could have won every dollar owned by the Fort Wayne sports; but I admit that I had so little confidence in myself that I would not have bet on thirty days' adherence to the Murphys. My associations were all with saloon keepers and gamblers. One of the former promised that if I kept the pledge one year, he would buy me a hat. The year is now nearly expired, and before this book is read I will be wearing a new hat at Jay Phillips' expense.

For the first few days I found my new life a hard one. I spent much of my time in saloons, playing cards for the drinks. When my companions took beer, I took a cigar; but the sight of the cool, foaming beverage which I loved so well, was a severe temptation, especially during those sultry days in August. Many times I found the pressure very strong, and was on the point of surrendering, but something within kept me on the track, and a still, small voice said to me, "Stick to it, Mace."

I soon came to the conclusion that if I remained in Fort Wayne, whisky would conquer. I could not in safety frequent my old places of resort, and therefore determined to attend the races at Geneseo, Ill., and at the same time visit some relatives living there, who are temperance and religious people. They were overjoyed to learn of the step I had taken, and gave me a hearty welcome. I remained at Geneseo ten days, during which time scarcely any temptation was thrown in my path. But I felt the old appetite tugging away at me, and the ungratified longing for liquor caused me much physical and mental distress. From Geneseo I went to Chicago, and there I met a number of my old companions, who were starting out to "make a night of it." Of course they insisted that I must go with them, and I consented to join the party. I knew I was taking a fearful risk, but I could not resist the invitation of my former chums. Few of my readers, perhaps, know what "making a night of it" in Chicago is. The term conveys a good deal. It means a night of dissipation and indulgence; it means hours spent in the heated atmosphere of the gilded palaces of vice, or the luxuriant abodes of sin; it means a gratification of the grossest appetites, and an indulgence in the basest pleasures; it means the robbing of sleep, the sacrifice of time, the waste of money, the injury to health, and the surrender of good name. "Making a night of it" has shattered some of the greatest intellects the world has ever known; has blighted the most promising careers; has wasted the most ample fortunes; has destroyed the happiness of the most affectionate families, and led to misery, and shame, and death, and eternal woe. There are thousands of young men who think it is manly to "make a night of it," but could they draw the lesson from the shattered remnants of manhood all over the land, could they see the depths of shame and remorse into which the devotee of the wine cup is finally plunged, could they know the misery caused by the fearful, insatiable craving for alcohol, could they hear the lamentations of the lost souls, sacrificed through the infernal love for spirits, not all the lights, and songs, and music, and good fellowship which surround vice with so many attractions, could lure them from the only path which leads to happiness, both in this world and in the world to come.

Well, we made a "night of it" in Chicago. I stayed with the "boys" until they reeled to their beds in drunken unconsciousness. I had not violated my pledge, having alternated between cigars and lemonade. At every "treat" I had taken one or the other; I had smoked several cigars, and given a number away, but when I reached my room I found that I had fifty-seven in my pocket. This will give the reader an idea of the liquor we drank, and the sum of money we squandered when we "made a night of it" in Chicago.

I was greatly pleased to think I had passed through this ordeal without breaking my pledge, and concluded that I was safe for the future. The next morning I avoided my associates of the previous night, for I found it no amusement to be with them unless I drank, and that I was determined not to do. I bought a few pools on the base ball games, lost as usual, and then started for Fort Wayne. Upon my return, I was besieged with questions, the most frequent one being, "Well, Mace, how many times were you drunk while you were gone?" Few were ready to believe me when I said that I had not tasted a drop since I left home. Some, however, cheered me with expressions of confidence, which encouraged me greatly; others — mostly gamblers and saloon keepers — asserted that I was playing a deep confidence game, my intentions being to worm myself into the confidence of the religious people of the city, and then borrow all the money I could and swindle them out of it. A gambler, who had for years been my " partner," made a charge of this kind quite publicly, and was rebuked by one of the Murphy leaders, who said, " I would lend Mace Long two hundred dollars for a year, without security, but I wouldn't lend you ten cents." This gentleman had never spoken to me, and when I heard of his kind expression I was greatly encouraged. The good people of the city aided me by many tokens of confidence and expressions of faith in my sincerity. Each day I found my resolutions stronger. I was still keeping a gambling room, and had as yet no higher ambition than to abstain from drinking, so as to make money at my illegitimate business. How I came to abandon my old calling and leave the paths I had so long trod for pleasanter and purer ones, I shall endeavor to tell in the next chapter.

CHAPTER IX.

MY CONVERSION TO THE GOSPEL OF JESUS CHRIST—MENTAL SUFFERINGS WHILE UNDER CONVICTION—PUBLIC CONFESSION OF MY SINS—THE BLESSINGS ATTENDING A CHANGE OF HEART.

Upon returning to Fort Wayne, I found that the temperance meetings, which were still in progress at the Rink, had a stronger attraction than ever for me. I discovered that the fascinations of the gambling table were losing their power, and I could take no interest in the games at my room. On the first night I went to the Rink, and the managers insisted that I should address the meeting; about fifteen hundred people were present, and the ordeal was a most trying one. I pleaded my "freshness," and had no idea that I could face that vast crowd without breaking down. But they kept calling for me, and I finally rose in my place and stated that I was unprepared to speak, but would make a few remarks upon some other occasion. Mr. Rusk then took the liberty of announcing that I would speak on the next evening, and at the same time stated that the number of signers had just reached six thousand.

This created much enthusiasm, and there was more signing and singing. I concluded not to attend the next evening, but was very lonesome, and my resolution failed me. I remained at my room until nine o'clock, but then almost involuntarily sought the "Old Ark." Hardly had I entered its portals when I heard my name shouted from all parts of the house, and in a moment I found myself standing upon the platform, with fifteen hundred upturned faces before me, and fifteen hundred pairs of eyes gazing intently upon me. I shook like an aspen leaf; my head fairly swam; a cold perspiration burst out all over me, and I could scarcely control my voice. I certainly suffered all the tortures of stage fright, and passed through an experience I never desire to repeat. But my self-possession soon returned, and after I had spoken a few words I was comparatively at ease. I told them, first of all, that I had been faithful to my pledge, taken several weeks before, and that I intended to adhere to it through life. I also related how I began drinking whisky; and how it had led me down from one depth to another, drawing me into other vices, until I had become a moral wreck, the mere plaything of a diabolical appetite. The next day my speech was printed in full in the papers. The press took more interest in me than ever, and chronicled my every movement. I knew that, under the circumstances, if I took a single misstep, it would be heralded to the world, and this made me more careful, perhaps, than I otherwise would have been, to adhere to my promises.

Having broken the ice, I spoke at the meetings nearly every night. I entered into the work with enthusiasm, and endeavored to gain recruits for the Murphy army. On the first afternoon I secured sixteen signers, among them a veteran whisky seller and whisky drinker, Mr. Arthur Dodge. I was greatly encouraged with my success. Mr. Dodge took hold of the work with much energy, and we canvassed together, inducing many old slaves of alcohol to don the blue ribbon, and emancipate themselves from the curse under which they had so long staggered.

For six weeks we labored night and day, with unvarying success. Then Messrs. Rusk and Reddick left us, and the whisky sellers concluded that the storm was about over, and that the meetings would soon "fizzle out." But we did not allow them to "fizzle." For four weeks we carried them on ourselves. Every man who took an interest in the cause came to the front, and we kept the enthusiasm constantly up to the boiling point. Our army was constantly increasing, and it looked as if we were to capture the entire city.

MASON LONG'S FIRST APPEARANCE AT THE RINK AT FORT WAYNE, IND.

At this stage of the movement, Messrs. Hallenbeck and Cassedy, who had been converted during the Moody-Sankey revival at Chicago, came among us, and took charge of the meetings, conducting them on the gospel temperance plan. Up to this date the Murphy movement had been carried on as a purely moral effort; now the religious element was with it, and the effect was good. The churches, many of which had held aloof, joined in with us. Hallenbeck and Cassedy remained five weeks, and were the means of accomplishing a vast amount of good. After their departure the meetings continued as usual, under the management of a board consisting of several of our best citizens. The Hon. Newton Burwell, a worthy Christian gentleman who has since entered the ministry, took the leadership.

Among the reformed men were a few who objected to the religious cast the movement had assumed. They organized a "Reformed Men's Club," and took control of the meetings, Mr. Burwell and the ministers retiring, but still giving the "boys" their sympathy and co-operation. An arrangement was then made by which strictly temperance meetings were held during the week, and a grand union prayer meeting every Sunday night. The interest deepened. Those who attended the Murphy meetings were sure to find their way to the

"Old Ark" on Sunday nights. By this means hundreds were brought within reach of the gospel, who had not heard it preached for years. A deep feeling pervaded the community. A great change was taking place in many of our reformed men.

They were beginning to inquire anxiously, "What shall we do to be saved?" They were thinking deeply of their future state, many of them for the first time, and recalling the lessons of childhood they had neglected for so many years. The long-forgotten Bible was hunted up, and its precious words were studied by men who had long been strangers to them; some who had objected most strenuously to the gospel work, now urged the propriety of a monster revival. We, therefore, sent for Dr. Earl, of Boston, a most successful evangelist. He came and conducted a series of meetings for three weeks, with grand results. The Rink was crowded every night; Dr. Earl expounded the Scriptures with singular power and eloquence, and led many poor sorrowing mortals into the way of salvation. He was assisted by the city pastors, and the religious people of Fort Wayne, and a most glorious harvest was reaped. Scores of converts were made. There was a grand awakening throughout the city. There was a most gracious outpouring of God's spirit, and many wayward hearts found peace in believing. As many as one hundred and eighty persons rose for prayer in a single meeting. Some of the most depraved men in the city tasted of the Bread of Life, and often "those who came to scoff remained to pray." This revival terminated the movement proper in Fort Wayne. The meetings had been held over three hundred consecutive nights, and ten thousand and seventeen persons had signed the pledge. A very small number of those who took the pledge violated it. A grand, noble, work had been accomplished; those who had been but a short year before in the gutters, or in the jails, their existence a curse to themselves and their families, were now "clothed, and in their right mind." Employment was obtained for them, and they became industrious and esteemed members of the community. Their families found peace and happiness in homes long abandoned to misery and despair, and thanked God that alcohol no longer claimed their protectors among its victims. A year ago, many of them looked forward only to the penitentiary, or the poor house; now, not a few cherish hopes of a happy future, and have their names enrolled on the books of the churches, of which they are attentive and consistent members. They have tasted the "pleasures" of this world, and know that they are all vanity. They mourn over their wasted years, and realize

what is charged against them in the book of
judgment. They are working now to balance
their accounts for the Last Great Day, and well
know that the consecration of the remainder
of their lives to purity and righteousness will
not atone for the sinfulness and folly of their
past. I sometimes think that these men, who
have been redeemed after careers of wickedness and crime, enjoy the love of God better
than the old followers of the Cross, who have
never tasted the bitter experience which is sure
to follow indulgence in the so-called "pleasures" of this world. Those of us who have
been saved, as if by fire, and "plucked like
brands from the burning," should strive to live
very near to God, for the change is so great, that
it will require all of our efforts to keep in the
straight and narrow path, which leads to eternal bliss. I shudder when I think where I and
so many others, who had drifted far out into
the currents of sin, would be now, but for
the glorious temperance movement which has
swept over the land, and snatched us up just
in time to save us from the abyss toward
which we were hastening. I can recall the
names of many poor fellows — my former companions — who have gone beyond our reach to
everlasting ruin, without a taste of the blessed
peace and happiness which have been so graciously vouchsafed to me. I feel deeply that

there is a great field for work among those whom the world considers outcasts. I know that in every human being, however depraved, there is the germ of some good, which may be reached and developed by prayer and striving, and I have solemnly vowed to consecrate the rest of my life to the work of rescuing these poor unfortunate creatures from the evil which surrounds them. I am endeavoring every day to speak the word which shall reveal to some wandering soul the light that I have found, and so long as God gives me life and strength, I shall persevere in my chosen work. I date my reformation from the hour I signed the temperance pledge. Previous to that time, I was greatly addicted to profanity, but since then an oath has never escaped my lips. I had always mingled with the dissipated, the depraved, and the vicious; but the Murphys brought me in contact with another and a better class of people. I formed the acquaintance of noble Christian men and women, who were endeavoring to illustrate, by their daily lives and conversation, the precepts of their blessed Master, and from them, I imbibed new conceptions of life, its duties and its realities. When I ceased to drink, and to swear, I found it comparatively easy to discard my numerous other vices one by one. I enjoyed daily a visible increase in my self respect. I began to feel as if I were a "man among men." The evil habits which had become a part of my very being, soon left me, all but gambling. That vice had an irresistible fascination for me. I loved the game above everything else; I did not think I could ever give it up. Besides, my moral faculties were so blunted, that I did not think it was wrong to gamble, provided it was done "on the square." I thought a man could be a professional gambler, and a respectable citizen at the same time, but I found out my mistake — they are incompatible.

My nightly attendance at the temperance meetings continued. I enjoyed them very much—in fact above everything else in the world; I listened to the experiences of the reformed men—frequently related with a remarkable simplicity and pathos; I repeatedly found myself in tears, as I heard their sad stories of sin and suffering; I often sat in the Rink and reflected upon my past life until I was so choked with emotion as not to be able to respond when called upon to speak.

This feeling was new to me and I could not comprehend it. There was a change taking place in myself which it puzzled me greatly to understand. For weeks I was in this condition. My only real enjoyment was during the temperance meetings. I could find no pleasure at the gaming-table, and, winner or loser, I always left it in disgust. The reader can realize the alteration in me when he remembers that for years the game of faro had cast a perfect spell over me ; that I had repeatedly played it for many hours at a time, unable to leave it for food or sleep, and only withdrawing when I could no longer bear the physical strain. But now the temperance meetings drew me from my game every evening, and the gambling-room had become the most repulsive place on earth to me.

Sunday is always the liveliest day for gamblers, for it is then they do their best business. It was so with me, but since my moral awakening I found Sunday the longest and dullest day of the week. One Sunday morning I resolved to attend divine service, and found my way to the First Baptist church. The sight of a notorious professional gambler in that sacred place startled the congregation, and every eye was turned upon me as the usher showed me to a seat. The pastor, Rev. Dr. J. R. Stone, preached a most beautiful and effective sermon, which seemed intended especially for me. I eagerly drank in every word, and as the good man continued, I found myself shedding tears of sorrow and remorse for my misspent life. After the sermon the choir sang "What shall the harvest be?" and as I listened to the beautiful music, all the sins of my past life seemed to pass in review before me. I had sown the crop, and I wondered what my harvest would be. As I was leaving the church my eyes rested upon the little lady, through whose kind words I had been led to sign the pledge. I thought this a happy omen. She handed me a Bible, saying that she had marked a lesson for me to study during the coming week, and asked if I would do so. I gladly promised her, and with the good book in my hand, I left the church and hastened to my room. There I found a big game of faro in progress, but I passed the players and went into my chamber, where I began to study the Bible which had been given me. Occasionally one of the gamblers would come into the room, and then I would secrete the book, as I feared ridicule. I spent many hours every day studying the word of God, and especially those pages which had been marked for me. I was constantly interrupted, and always hid the book. One day I was caught fairly and squarely by one of the gamblers. He was greatly surprised, and his remarks ran about like this:

"Hallo, what is that? a Bible? well I declare, old boy, you're gone, sure. You're no longer the same man that you was before you signed the Murphy pledge than any thing in the world. There's no more fun in you any more; a fellow might just as well talk to a cigar sign as to try to get a word out of you.

You've Bible on the brain. You'll be crazy as a bed-bug in less than a month. Drop your d—d nonsense, Mace, and I'll show you a new thing in card playing. I'm playing colors now, and it will win sure, and no one shall stand in with this but you."

These words made no impression upon my mind. I was greatly troubled, but not about faro. I read and re-read my Bible lesson, and the more I pondered it the greater became my mental anxiety. In despair I laid down the book, went to the gambling table, and tried to interest myself at faro. It was useless; the old charm had vanished; the old spell was broken. I left the table in disgust and resumed my Bible reading, but could find no peace. Night and day my torture increased. Sleep was a stranger to my eyelids and the food, at every meal, remained untasted before me. I began to think the gambler was right when he told me that I would go crazy, for my faculties seemed to be shaken. I left the city, but after a day's absence I returned. I felt an insatiable craving for something, I knew not what, a want which I could not define nor comprehend, but which was ever present.

My condition physically was almost as bad as it was mentally. I was weak, restless, and feverish, and therefore consulted a physician, who told me that I was threatened with serious illness, and prescribed for me. But his medicine did not reach the vital spot. Under its effects I slept, but I had troubled dreams, and when I rose I was neither rested nor refreshed. For several days and nights I had neither slept nor eaten. I was under conviction, and felt that my sins, which were as scarlet, could never be forgiven. I looked forward to a life of woe, and anxiously inquired of those I met what I should do.

"Put your trust in God," they would say.

"But I do trust Him. I have given up everything, and tried to be a Christian; but I can't. I can find no peace; I feel as if my God had forsaken me, and that there is no salvation for such as I."

My mental condition was worse than ever. I longed to get away from myself — to fly to some distant solitude, some trackless forest—to any place that I could find peace. I frequently tried to pray, but the words seemed to mock me. Discouraged and hopeless, I sought my old companions, and sought to be one of them again. It was useless. Their profane words grated on my ears; their coarse jokes and jests were intensely painful to me. The club room and saloons were abominable in my sight, and I avoided them as much as possible.

And so my life wore on. If my sins had been great, so had my sufferings. It would take a genius to portray my mental torments. I realized that no human being could successfully "minister to a mind diseased," and the Great Physician seemed to have forsaken me. Sometimes I would rise from my knees after a long season of prayer, with a happier feeling and with tears streaming from my eyes. Then I would think that the Lord had forgiven me, and granted me His blessing; but when I went to my club room, the old feeling of despair came back to me with redoubled force.

Sabbath came again, and in company with Brother Hallenbeck I attended the Wayne Street Methodist-Episcopal church, and heard the pastor, Rev. R. N. McKaig, deliver a sermon to reformed men. The discourse was an able one, and I enjoyed it very much, but did not get the relief I craved.

After leaving the church, I told my troubles to Brother Hallenbeck. I told him the mental anguish and physical exhaustion I was suffering; how hard I was trying to become a Christian, and how useless the effort seemed; how I had prayed God for hours at a time to forgive my sins and grant me a new heart, but He had denied me the blessing I asked; how for seven days I had neither eaten nor slept, but had passed through the most fearful experience of my life.

Brother Hallenbeck listened attentively to

me, and expressed deep sympathy with me. He tried to encourage me, and said there was evidently something I had left undone. He did not know what it was, but he thought if I would go to the Rink that evening, publicly confess before the audience that I was a great sinner, and declare my faith in Christ, I would find peace.

I told him I would take his advice, and hoped it would bring me consolation. I spent the afternoon in my room, trying to think what I would say at the Rink. When I left for the meeting, I thought I knew exactly what I would say, but I changed my mind a dozen times ere I reached the building.

I entered and took a seat beside the speakers — Hon. Wm. McConnell and Mrs. Jesse M. Gale, of Angola. There were about fifteen hundred people present, and two grand speeches were made. I could, however, take little interest in them, for I felt the old gnawing at my soul, and the old burden upon my mind.

When the speakers had concluded and the audience was about to disperse, Mr. Hallenbeck announced that I, at my own request, would speak a few words. The people looked surprised, and, as many were tired, I felt as if they regarded me in the light of an interloper. However, I hastened to the rostrum, anxious not to delay the audience, and longing to unburden myself. When I faced the vast assemblage, I could not remember a word that I had intended to say. However, I found language — I think God gave it to me — and this is what I said, as reported in the newspapers next day:

"A few months ago I stood upon this rostrum and confessed that I was a drunkard. Now I want to make another confession, which is, that I am a great sinner. For the past ten days and nights I have not enjoyed one hour's natural sleep, so deep is my conviction, and my burden of sin is so great that I can live this way no longer. So I have come to you for help. Oh! I want to beg the Christian people of Fort Wayne to pray for me, that I may find rest. I have been praying all this time, but my prayers are not answered. I have been constantly reading my Bible, and the more I study it the greater is my distress. In it I have found a passage which troubles me greatly. It is this: 'For we must all appear before the judgment seat of Christ, that every one may receive the things done in the body, according to that he hath done, whether it be good or bad.' —(2 Corinthians x, 5.) These words continually sounded in my ears, and led me to sum up my case as it would be on the Last Great Day. I wondered what good I had done in this world, and tried to balance it against the evil, but the latter sent it up to the beam; the account would not balance. I consulted the Revs. Stone, Moffatt, McKaig, McFarland, and others, and they kindly advised me. I told them I was guilty, and I now plead guilty before the Great Judge and these witnesses. I am a poor, miserable sinner, but hope for God's mercy, and I feel that my dear sainted mother is interceding in my behalf."

When I sat down I was in tears, but I felt greatly relieved. Many were weeping in the audience; for indeed the scene was an affecting one. I, who had been a professional gambler, saloon keeper, and drunkard; who had for years violated not only divine but human laws; who had been regarded by all as a reckless, degraded character; who had run the gauntlet of sin — stood up before fifteen hundred Christian people, and asked their prayers for my salvation. The spectacle was certainly an extraordinary one.

After my remarks, Dr. Stone was called upon to pray for me. He said if there were others who, like me, were seeking the way to Christ, and desired to be remembered in the prayer, they should stand up. All over the house strong men rose to their feet, many in tears, and the seal of conviction upon their faces. Dr. Stone prayed for me and the other stricken souls with an unction and fervor which were wonderful.

The prayer was a marvel and every word of it sank deep into my heart. It was a thrilling and powerful appeal for mercy, and I shall remember it to my dying day. I believe God heard and answered it.

I returned to my room, fell on my knees and implored God to hear me in my distress. Then I retired and laid awake, thinking of the same old subject until two o'clock, when I arose, turned on the gas, and looked about me. I stepped into the club room, and looked at the gambling tables, the sideboard, and all the appurtenances, and then asked myself, "Why should God forgive me while I remain in this place, where I have never done aught but sin against Him." Gambling was my favorite vice, and I had never yet determined to abandon it. But then a sudden resolution was formed; I took one last look at the gambling room, at the faro table, where I had played so often—at the sideboard from which I had repeatedly dealt out whisky to my fellow men—and then quit the place forever. It was then and there that I made the complete surrender to Christ as every one must do, who desires to be saved.

I went to a hotel, took a room, and again sought my Maker. In less than an hour I felt that the blessing had come which I had striven for so long. I went to bed and the pillow was soon wet with tears which were streaming from my eyes—tears, not of sorrow and remorse, but of joy and gladness. I at once fell asleep and enjoyed unbroken slumber. The next morning I awoke with a light heart. The sun was shining brightly into my room and it seemed as if I had never seen such a beautiful morning before. I looked out of the window and saw a clear, cloudless sky, a fit image of the condition of my soul after so many days of anguish and torture.

I hurried from the room to tell my Christian friends that their prayers had been answered, and the verdict had come. I was so happy that I wanted all the world to share my joy.

I had at last found peace, and truly it was the peace that passeth all understanding. I was hopeful of a bright future and an eternity of bliss. None who have not passed through the same blessed experience that I have, can realize what a great change there was in my life and feelings, and thoughts. I found a new charm in living, a new beauty in nature, a new light in the world. I was cheerful and was greeted with an encouraging smile by all who met me. I consecrated myself to Christ and solemnly vowed to devote the remainder of my life to His service. I now bless God every day and every hour for His infinite mercy and goodness to me. I am striving constantly to bring other wandering souls to Him, that they may, like me, find peace in believing.

CHAPTER X.

MY ADMISSION INTO THE FIRST BAPTIST CHURCH OF FORT WAYNE—IMMERSION IN THE PRESENCE OF A VAST AUDIENCE—PRESS REPORTS OF THE CEREMONY.

It is utterly impossible for me to describe the vast change that had taken place in me since my conversion. My entire being seemed to have undergone a transformation, and my life, feelings, thoughts, impulses, and ambitions had been completely altered. I no longer felt the slightest desire to tread the paths I had so long traveled; the so-called pleasures of this world had lost all their charms for me. My only desire was to do that which should be pleasing in the sight of the Lord and bring down upon me His blessings, and approval.

The question of identifying myself with some church, early presented itself to my mind, and I deliberated over it carefully. I felt deeply my own unworthiness, and it seemed to me that it would involve an undue degree of assurance for me to present myself as a candidate for public admission into the ranks of God's professed disciples. In so doing I would take upon myself vows, the force and sacredness of which I fully recognized. What church, thought I, will care to welcome me to its folds, until I bring forth "fruits meet for repentance," and prove by my daily life and conversation, that I am entirely sincere in my professions, and earnest in my declared intentions of leading a purer and nobler life? What church will have confidence enough in me to take the risk of my future being such as, not only not to dishonor myself, but to cast a stigma upon its name, and bring reproach upon the cause of our Blessed Master? These doubts were continually arising and I remained undecided for some time as to what course to pursue.

On the other hand I felt a strong yearning to enroll my name upon the books of some congregation, and become entirely affiliated with God's people. I longed to sit at the communion table, and in company with old followers of the Cross partake of the blessed sacrament which the Savior ordained. I felt that if I obtained a recognized place in the Christian community, I could enjoy the manifold blessings of religion, as I could never do if I remained outside the pale of the church, and I finally determined — despite the doubts to which I have referred and to which I gave full weight — to apply for admission to the membership of some religious organization.

This conclusion was only arrived at after

repeated consultations with my trusted and beloved spiritual adviser, Dr. Stone. He advised me to join some church promptly, believing it to be not only my duty, but a glorious privilege of which I should not hesitate to avail myself. The serious step I had resolved upon — for I fully comprehended its solemnity and importance — was taken with prayerful deliberation and earnest reflection. I realized that there were hundreds of eyes upon me; that I was made the subject of much unfriendly comment, carping criticism, and unfavorable prediction; and that I must act with due circumspection and discretion. I studied my Bible with great care, and aimed to inform myself as to the duties and obligations of a professing Christian, in order to make sure that I could faithfully discharge them. I was also in doubt as to what denomination I should select, until I had read the third chapter of St. Matthew and the first chapter of St. Mark, including the following passages:

"And it came to pass in those days that Jesus came from Nazareth of Galilee, and was baptized of John in Jordan.

"And straightway coming up out of the water, He saw the heavens opened, and the Spirit like a dove descending upon Him.

"And there came a voice from the heavens

saying, 'Thou art my beloved son, in whom I am well pleased.' "—MARK i., 9, 10, 11.

Besides I found the Apostle Paul in his Epistle to the Romans (ch. vi., 4) speaking of baptism as "a *burial with Christ into death*," and a " rising with Him " to newness of life — and this seemed to settle the question as to what the ordinance was, in those days, as to its outward form.

These passages left no doubt in my mind as to the course I should pursue. I decided to unite with the Baptist Church, believing that as our Lord and Savior, Jesus Christ, had been baptized in the River Jordan, and had thereby called out a blessing from heaven, His disciple could not do better than to follow in His footsteps. I think that Jesus, by undergoing immersion exhibited a preference for that form of baptism, and that He is well pleased when His followers imitate His example in this as in other respects. I believe that were He on earth to-day, He would be a Baptist; and although that is my conviction, I have the deepest love and sympathy with professing Christians of all denominations, and am ready at all times to extend the right hand of fellowship to every human being, who may be striving, under any name, to advance the cause of righteousness and bring men to a saving knowledge of the gospel of Christ Jesus.

I communicated to Dr. Stone my desire to unite with his church (the First Baptist) at which he seemed highly gratified, although he said he desired me to act solely upon my own free will and my conviction of right and duty, and not through any partiality toward him or by reason of any undue influence he might possess over me. I satisfied him that my desire was the result of study and reflection, and on Friday evening, January 4, 1878, I offered myself as a candidate for Christian baptism and membership in the First Baptist Church of Fort Wayne at their regular covenant meeting.

What was expected of me here I could hardly conceive; as I had never before attended such a meeting, and knew almost nothing of the exercises appropriate to such an occasion, or the special significance of its peculiar name, much less the character and value of "*The Covenant Meeting.*"

As I have since been frequently asked, as to what sort of a meeting it is, and what is it like, perhaps some of my readers would be glad to have my description and estimate of it.

Covenant meetings, so called, are found, I believe, only among the Baptists, yet they are not very much unlike the general "class meetings" of the Methodist Church, in their general character. The pastor usually presides. After suitable opening devotional exercises, every member present is expected to speak, with more or less fullness, of personal religious experiences during the previous month or more, since last in attendance upon such an occasion; and especially to express each one's sense of obligation to the covenant vows entered into at the time of being received into membership; as also the strength and heartiness of one's attachment to the cause of Christ as a whole; and to the church and its respective membership in particular. In this line of thought, and toward these aims, all, without distinction or exception, are desired to speak, though it should be but in the briefest manner. Sometimes one hundred persons or more will "speak to the covenant" in the course of an hour and a quarter. These brief and unstudied utterances of religious experience, sometimes joyous and at other times sad and sorrowful, are almost always specially worth hearing; and sometimes they are eminently practical, thoughtful, suggestive, and profitable; and the pastor, by a suitable song, or scripture passage, or pertinent remarks interspersed, not only prevents a monotonous weariness, or a pointless, profitless, sameness of impression, but gives to the whole unity and variety as well; and freshness, vitality and interest; conducing to increased spirituality of mind, to vigorous growth of faith; to the strengthening of hope; the deepening and broadening of Christian experience and the stronger attachment of the members to one another and to the church.

The Baptists profess to take the Bible as their fundamental statute book and authority for all religious belief and practice in their several churches and their sovereign law for all ends, ways, and courses of life.

They publish to the world, however, a declaration of faith embracing eighteen different articles, with ample scriptural authority for the same. That all may know, if they desire, in how many and what things, they agree with other Christian people and in what respect they differ, I give the first and last of these declarations:

"I.—OF THE SCRIPTURES.

"We believe that the Holy Bible was written by men divinely inspired, and is a perfect treasure of heavenly instruction; that it has God for its author, salvation for its end, and truth without any mixture of error for its matter; that it reveals the principles by which God will judge us; and therefore is, and shall remain to the end of the world, the center of Christian union, and the supreme standard by which all human conduct, creeds, and opinions should be tried."

"XVIII.—OF THE WORLD TO COME.

"We believe that the end of the world is approaching; that at the last day Christ will descend from heaven, and raise the dead from the grave to final retribution; that a solemn separation will then take place; that the wicked will be adjudged to endless punishment, and the righteous to endless joy, and that this judgment will fix forever the final state of men in heaven or hell, on principles of righteousness."

In addition to this declaration of faith, they have, of course, certain by-laws and rules of order for the proper transaction of business, such as no one can object to, and also the following "covenant," to which every person joining the church is required to give his or her solemn pledge.

CHURCH COVENANT.

"Having been led, as we believe, by the Spirit of God, to receive the Lord Jesus Christ as our Savior, and on the profession of our faith, having been baptized in the name of the Father, and of the Son, and of the Holy Ghost, we do now, in the presence of God, angels, and this assembly, most solemnly and joyfully enter into covenant with one another, as one body in Christ.

"We engage, therefore, by the aid of the Holy Spirit, to walk together in Christian love; to strive for the advancement of this church in knowledge, holiness, and comfort; to promote its prosperity and spirituality; to sustain its worship, ordinances, discipline, and doctrines; to contribute cheerfully and regularly to the support of the ministry, the expenses of the church, the relief of the poor, and the spread of the gospel through all nations.

"We also engage to maintain family and secret devotions; to religiously educate our children; to seek the salvation of our kindred and acquaintances; to walk circumspectly in the world; to be just in our dealings, faithful in our engagements, and exemplary in our deportment; to avoid all tattling, back-biting, and excessive anger; to abstain from the sale and use of intoxicating drinks as a beverage, and to be zealous in our efforts to advance the kingdom of our Savior.

"We further engage to watch over one another in brotherly love; to remember each other in prayer; to aid each other in sickness and distress; to cultivate Christian sympathy in feeling and courtesy of speech; to be slow to take offense, but always ready for reconciliation, and mindful of the rules of our Savior, to secure it without delay.

"We moreover engage, that when we remove from this place, we will as soon as possible unite with some other church, where we can carry out the spirit of this covenant, and the principles of God's word."

It will be at once perceived that every member of any Baptist Church professes, and is believed to be a spiritually renewed person—regenerated or "born again" of the Holy Spirit—fully resolved and determined, by the help and grace of God, to live an upright, honest, pure, and consistent Christian life—every one being also most solemnly "*pledged to total abstination from all intoxicating drinks as a beverage*" both as to the sale and personal use—and in all things determined with full purpose of heart to adorn the doctrine of God our Savior, and so to glorify the Lord Jesus; and to "*save the perishing*" as best they can. Their professions and aims are good. May their endeavors and their outward lives be always found to correspond.

It was after reading this "church covenant" and all the members present, perhaps forty or fifty in all, had spoken, that the pastor, Dr. Stone, asked me if I desired to present myself for membership. Upon signifying my wish to be a member among them, I was asked to tell the church in my own way, the dealings of God with my soul, especially as to my change of heart and life, my new thoughts and feelings, my purposes and aims, my spirit, my hopes, my faith, my knowledge of God and the way of salvation from the power, the love, the dominion and the condemnation of sin. With great hesitancy and much trembling and self distrust, I told them as best I could—under the circumstances—the substance of what I have sincerely written out for this little book, found in Chapter nine. It was, of course, not so conveniently put together at the time—and some of it came out by question and answer; but I have already given you the essential substance of what, at that time, I tried to say briefly.

I then related my Christian experience, told how I had been led, as I firmly believed, by the Spirit of God, to receive the Lord Jesus Christ as my Savior, how the change of heart for which I had prayed, came to me in the night, only after I had made a complete surrender of my worldly vices, and bade farewell to the gambling table forever, how I had drawn the bolt of the door of my soul, where the Master had been rapping for admission so many years, but in vain, how with the change of heart had come the feeling of peace and rest to which I had ever been a stranger, and how I had new and warm impulses of kindness and compassion for my fellow men to whose salvation I had vowed to devote the remainder of my life.

After these remarks, I was requested to retire, and in a few moments my pastor joined me and told me I had been unanimously chosen to membership.

Nine or ten days elapsed before my immersion. Several unauthorized announcements of the ceremony appeared in the daily papers, which had the effect of filling the church on each occasion. It was hardly necessary to say that the publications were not made for this purpose, as falsely claimed by some. The eventful evening finally came, and the ceremony was performed in the presence of a vast assemblage. I append extracts from the accounts printed in two of the daily papers of Fort Wayne.

[*From The News, Jan.* 14, 1878.]

"BURIED IN BAPTISM.—MASON LONG TAKES UPON HIMSELF A NEW LIFE.

"Last evening, long before the usual hours for service, the First Baptist Church on West Jefferson Street was thronged with an earnest and interested assemblage, that had come together to witness the solemn ordinances of baptism. The candidates consisted of one lady and three gentlemen, among the latter, Mr. Mason Long, so well and favorably known as one of the best hearted and most generous men in the community, who has lately turned from a life of pure and unadulterated cussedness to a higher and nobler existence, and whose sincere and honest profession can not but be fruitful of lasting good in the community. Mr. Long's example may safely be imitated by hundreds of his former companions in worldly life and pleasures. His address to the congregation was a manly confession of a stricken and contrite heart, and his words sank deep into the souls of the immense assemblage. Moistened eyes, many of them unused to weeping, were observed on all sides, and silent prayers from hundreds of sympathetic hearts were sent upward for the new converts' continued faith and final glorious exchange of the church militant for the church triumphant. The remarks of Rev. Dr. Stone were peculiarly appropriate to the occasion, his welcome to the candidates was cordial, and the impression made upon the vast audience was deeply impressive."

[*From the Sentinel, same day.*]

"BORN AGAIN — THE ORDINANCE OF BAPTISM ADMINISTERED TO MASON LONG AND OTHERS LAST EVENING.

"The *Sentinel*, on Saturday last, having given notice that the rite of Baptism would be administered last evening at the First Baptist Church, a large congregation greeted the candidates; in fact as early as seven o'clock, the large auditorium of this beautiful church was filled, and every foot of available standing room was crowded. The sensation of the hour was the baptism of the well-known temperance orator, Mr. Mason Long, whose remarkable conversion from a life of more concentrated cussedness to the square foot, than perhaps any other member of the community, to an entirely new, and, it is to be hoped, holier existence, has caused such a profound sensation. That his changed life and his concomitant professions are sincere, no real friend and well wisher hesitates to believe; the skeptical are found in the ranks of those who miss his presence and patronage, and remember him as their former friend and boon companion. Mr. Long connected himself with the temperance movement last August, and, having thus evinced a desire to reform, became the subject of much solicitude and the target of many heartfelt invocations to God, that he might be endowed with strength and courage to overcome the habits that seemed to have completely, and it was feared irrevocably, fastened upon him. Kind counsels, Christian arguments prevailed; and from good to better Mace has gone on until he finds himself within the folds of a Christian Church, with vows registered aloft to well and truly live so that when he is called to exchange worlds he can die in full hopes of a blessed immortality.

"After the usual preliminary services, the Rev. J. R. Stone, pastor, called upon Mr. Long to say a few words, that the immense auditory could see that he understood the ordinance so soon to be administered, and that he had, after much prayerful meditation and mature deliberation, voluntarily accepted it with all its kindred obligations. The assemblage was hushed to complete silence as he spoke the following words:

"'How thankful I am that I have been spared to help make this scene. I am thankful that I can stand before you and claim Christ as my Savior. Only a few months ago I came to this house with a bleeding heart, and with tears of remorse and sorrow for my past wicked life. I listened to a sermon, every word of which seemed especially intended for me, and

I eagerly drank in the sweet music, which made my heart beat as it never had before. After the service one of the Sabbath-school scholars of the church came to me with a Bible, with many passages marked for me as my lesson; why she gave me this book God only knows. I went to my room and studied my lesson. I was convicted and one month thereafter went to the Rink, stood up before hundreds of people, confessed my sins, and asked God to forgive them. Then I went to my room seeking rest, but found none. Looking at the gambling apparatus for the last time, I left the room at two o'clock at night, went to a hotel, and found rest.

"'I again asked God's forgiveness, and then recalled the promise to my dying mother, that I would be a good boy and meet her in heaven. How well I remember her last words, "God have mercy on my boy." Those are sweet words to me, and I am very thankful that they are yet fresh in my memory. I have one request to make of the Christian people; that is, to pray for me earnestly, as I go down into the pool, that the dark past may be washed away forever, and that I may come up praising the Lord forever and forever.

"'May I say one word to my pastor: You have watched over me for years. I have shunned you time and again. When under the influence of liquor I have frequently met you in the streets, when my guilty conscience would drive me into an alley or saloon, where I knew you would not follow, and for this I now ask your forgiveness. I have prayed for God to allow you to remain with us for many years to come, as our pastor, and should it be your lot to be called from us, when you are standing with the angels above you will not forget your little flock on earth.'

"There were few dry eyes among the audience upon the conclusion of the address, which was delivered in a feeling manner that appealed directly to the consciences of all present."

I have never regretted for one moment the step I took upon that memorable evening. As I emerged from the pool, I felt all my good purposes strengthen and my determination never to bring dishonor or disgrace upon the cause of Christ, was more fixed than ever. The solemn and beautiful rite of baptism seemed to bring a blessing with it, and to inspire me with new courage and increased confidence, in the great conflict I had undertaken. I have succeeded in fulfilling my solemn pledges, and in leading a consistent, upright, Christian life. I have prayerfully sought, by word and action, to glorify the Lord, who hath done such great things for me, and I believe that by His blessing, I have been the humble instrument of accomplishing some good. I am ready and willing to do whatsoever my hands can find, and I esteem it an especial comfort and privilege that I am able to labor in the Lord's vineyard. I feel deeply my own unworthiness, but have an abiding faith in the grace of God, that it will remain with me to the end. I am active in the church, and in the temperance cause, and my only regret is that it is not in my power to do all that I would like to, bringing perishing souls to a knowledge of Christ Jesus, and inducing poor sinful human beings to embrace the glorious salvation which is free to all.

CHAPTER XI.

MY CAREER SINCE MY CONVERSION—WHAT I AM DOING IN THE TEMPERANCE WORK.

"How shall I gain my livelihood" was a question of great importance to me, after I had entered upon my new life. I had but a limited education, little knowlege of any trade or business, and in addition to these disadvantages, I was penniless, and embarrassed by debts aggregating a considerable amount. I was, however, greatly encouraged by some of our best citizens and most prominent business men, who voluntarily sought me out, and asked me what occupation I desired to engage in, at the same time promising me their assistance and support. Among them was Mr. John D. Olds, a wealthy gentleman, who with true Christian generosity, said to me: "I want you to pick out a business that you are capable of doing, and you shall not lack for the means to carry it on." This noble offer was thankfully accepted, and I speedily availed myself of Mr. Olds' kindness. I rented a building in Fort Wayne, fitted it up, and in one week opened a temperance restaurant, for ladies and gentlemen. The "Model Coffee House," as I called it, was made neat and attractive, and at once became very popular, among the best classes of people. Many, no doubt, have patronized me by way of encouragement, and for this I am very thankful. My business has been uniformly good since I began. Some days as many as two hundred and twenty-five meals have been taken in my place. Among those who have patronized me, were saloon keepers and sporting men, who have encouraged me in my new life, and expressed regret that they too could not muster up courage to take the step I had taken. I have endeavored to induce them to abandon their evil ways, and lead better lives, and have succeeded in getting a great many drunkards to sign the pledge, and become men among men. I got fifty-nine of the very worst of that class, to put on the blue ribbon, in one month, and with scarcely an exception, they are faithful to their promises. Among the most staunch and determined in their new mode of life, are those who, like me, have drained the cup of dissipation and vice to its dregs, and become satisfied that the inevitable fruits of such indulgence are shame, sorrow, and distress.

I soon found out that "it pays to be a man." I made many warm friends, in my new pursuit, and received offers of pecuniary assistance from persons who had scarcely ever exchanged a word with me. These unsolicited proofs of confidence, gratified me beyond measure, and I am striving to prove myself worthy of them.

After my conversion, I received a great many invitations to visit neighboring towns and speak on the question of temperance. I am no orator, and have not enjoyed the advantages of an education, but I go and tell the story of my wrecked but redeemed life, and it seems to have as much effect as the most eloquent and polished speech. I make no pretensions, and am neither working for fame nor money. I am willing—nay, anxious—to go wherever I can accomplish even the smallest amount of good. I have usually had large audiences, and have received abundant testimony that my labors have not been wholly fruitless. I have delivered over one hundred addresses in the year which has elapsed since I consecrated myself to this work. In Toledo I spoke to an audience of fourteen hundred, and on the next evening I went into the country and talked to one hundred and fifty people. On the 31st of last May, I spoke at the great Murphy gathering of ten thousand persons, at Logansport, and on the succeeding evening I went to a small village, eighteen miles from Fort Wayne, where the first saloon was about to be started. I spoke in the church to a small gathering, among those present being the two young men who had left their farms in order to open this saloon. I told in my plain and humble way, what whisky had done for me, and these young men, after the speech, came forward and signed the pledge. They gave up the saloon idea and went back to the farm. Although my audience numbered but sixty-five, I went away with a light heart, feeling that I had done more good than at Logansport, where I had ten thousand listeners. I have spoken at large meetings in Chicago, Terre Haute, and many other cities. Among the places that I have delivered speeches are Elkhart, Valparaiso, Warsaw, Larville, Monroeville, Columbia City, Logansport, Lafayette, Peru, Wabash, Huntington, Roanoke, Delphi, Saline City, Defiance, Napoleon, Antwerp, Decatur, Bluffton, Auburn, Waterloo, Angola, Kendallville, Ligonier, La Otto, Cherubusco, Muuson's Chapel, Van Wert, Coldwater, Ann Arbor, Ypsilanti, and many others. At several of these points I have spoken twice; some three times, and once (South Bend) as many as seven times.

I am not telling my story, or traveling through the country, in order to make a living. My little restaurant business at Fort Wayne supports me, and I have no desire to gain a livelihood by my efforts in the cause of temperance. Usually, when I speak, a collection is taken up, and the proceeds handed to me. I make a practice of deducting my necessary expenses, and donating the remainder to the organization under whose auspices I may be speaking. Most of these associations are poor, and need this money, and I think much good is done by these contributions. I speak of this, not to take any credit to myself, but merely to disabuse the public of the idea, which is very prevalent, that every man who travels about in the temperance cause does so from mercenary motives. I think my plan is the best, and that if all who are interested in this great movement would adopt it, the general results would be better.

In my labors in this field, I make no efforts at eloquence or rhetorical flourish. I simply tell my story in plain, unadorned language, such as I have used in this book, and I believe the effect is usually good. I especially try, in my humble way, to influence the children. I believe that everything in this life depends upon getting the right kind of a start, and that in nine cases out of ten, those who fall into evil courses, and become intemperate and licentious, do so from the failure to receive proper training in childhood. I have never doubted that my career would have been widely different, but for the adverse surroundings of my youth. I think it is a wise policy for children to sign this pledge, and become interested in this great movement. The influence of the little people in this world is, I think, largely under-estimated. If directed into the right channels, they are able to exert a vast power for good; and a great mistake is made when we overlook them in organizing the work of reform.

I sometimes think that parents, as a rule, do not comprehend the fearful responsibilities under which they labor. They have precious, immortal souls, intrusted to their care, and they should see to it that these great trusts are properly discharged. The social glass of wine, the friendly game of cards in the home circle, may seem very innocent pastimes; but in how many children have they implanted the fondness for gambling, or the taste for liquor, which has afterward proved their ruin? The effect of these things is not, I think, sufficiently understood by fathers and mothers; and I esteem it part of my mission to open their eyes, so far as it is in my power, to the awful consequences which they invite by their thoughtlessness and carelessness.

My story is finished. I give my little book to the world, painfully aware that it is deficient in literary merit, and that the cultured and educated may subject its pages to the most severe, but doubtless deserved, criticism. For this I am fully prepared. But I cherish a lingering hope that this unpretending little volume, in spite of its many and acknowledged faults, may be the means of doing some little good; that the story of my wasted life may prove a warning to some who are just entering upon the pathway I trod so many years; and that others who, like me, have drifted far out into the current of sin and wickedness, may be led by my blessed experience to seek the Savior, and find the peace and happiness which are now denied them.

And now I bid farewell to my readers, and may God bless them all.

TESTIMONIALS FROM CLERGYMEN.

From Rev. J. R. Stone, D.D., Pastor First Baptist Church, Fort Wayne, Ind.

FORT WAYNE, July 5, 1878.

TO WHOMSOEVER THIS MAY COME:

This is to Certify, That Mr. Mason Long is a member of the First Baptist Church, Fort Wayne, Indiana, in good and regular standing, and that he has the full confidence and fellowship of our entire membership. We regard him as a truly reformed, honest, worthy man, and a sincere Christian, as he is also an earnest, effective worker in the temperance cause. As such we commend him. J. R. STONE,

Pastor First Baptist Church.

From Rev. Samuel Haskell, D.D., Pastor First Baptist Church, Ann Arbor, Michigan.

ANN ARBOR, May 30, 1878.

MR. MASON LONG — *My Dear Brother:* Absence from home, and illness, have prevented my writing sooner, to say what I have desired to since your labors in our city and vicinity. It is due to you, and to the cause at large, that we bear our testimony to the excellent effect of your addresses, and personal bearing among us. While all Christian people have taken you to their hearts in liveliest sympathy, and continued prayerful remembrance, many others, who had distrusted or feared the Christian element in our reform, have been brought to a wiser thoughtfulness. If an experience of the religion of Christ can do that of which you are a witness, hardened and prejudiced men must feel that they should think again before rejecting it, or disavowing its power in recovering the lost.

May God keep and strengthen you, making you a still brighter and everlasting "epistle written in the heart, known and read of all men."

Your audience here was the best of any weekly assembly which our year of remarkable meetings and eminent speakers had witnessed.

Most sincerely yours,

SAMUEL HASKELL.

From Rev. H. A. Gobin, D.D., Pastor First Methodist Church, Lafayette, Indiana.

LAFAYETTE, May 13, 1878.

MR. MACE LONG—*Dear Brother:* I was not permitted to hear you on your former visit to Lafayette, but as I listened to you last night, I was not surprised at the wonderful sensation and blessed influence pervading our city on the occasion of your first address in our temperance meetings. The recital of your experience is one of the most pathetic and satisfying testimonies to the value of Christianity that I ever heard. May God bless you, my brother. You ought to spend your whole time in telling the story of your eventful life. Your zeal in sin almost ruined you, but your zeal in righteousness will not only bless your own heart, but by the blessing of God you can save thousands from the gulf of misery to which you were hastening.

Several of our most intelligent citizens have remarked to me that your address was the most impressive appeal for temperance and religion they ever heard. For years and years you will be gratefully remembered in Lafayette. May you never do a thing to cast a shadow on our esteem and love for you. We all say, may God bless Mace Long. Cordially your brother,

H. A. GOBIN.

From Rev. Robert MacKenzie, D.D., Pastor First Presbyterian Church, Lafayette, Indiana.

LAFAYETTE, April 30, 1878.

MASON LONG, ESQ.—*My Christian Brother:* Let me assure you of the great good your words have done in our midst in awakening more of the spirit of the gospel in our temperance work in Lafayette. All the workers have been encouraged and refreshed by your visit. As for myself I can only repeat words I said to my congregation on the subject: "I have sat at the feet of seven professors for seven years, to fit myself to stand in the pulpit, but in the experiences of the human heart, in the spirit necessary to reach those who have wandered far from God, in the subduing, sweetening influence of the gospel upon such hearts, I learned something from the related experience of Mace Long which I never learned from a professor, and which has greatly helped me to follow the Master in saving the outcast and the prodigal. And he was all the better teacher because he did not know he was instructing us who sat at his back on the platform."

May God bless you, my brother, and keep you humble and near the Cross. May God bless the Blue Ribbon movement that caught you in your downward way. Be faithful to the end if only for the dear mother's sake whose last pulse was a prayer for her boy.

Yours in Christian temperance,
ROBERT MACKENZIE.

CHAPTER XII.

A SUPPLEMENTARY CHAPTER WRITTEN BY MY PASTOR, AT MY REQUEST.

My acquaintance with Mr. Long began in 1869. I had noticed in my congregation, soon after entering upon my pastorate in Fort Wayne, a gentleman of pleasing countenance and genteel appearance, who seemed to be a stranger to my people, and yet not a little interested in the services. He came again and again. I soon learned that he was known in town as "a sporting man," and was a skillful manipulator of cards, and regarded as a lucky, plucky, jolly good fellow. I would sometimes miss him from church for awhile, and was told that he was away on business; perhaps at "the Races," which he followed from New Orleans to Saratoga; or at some county or State fair, plying his "profession;" but if in the city, which he called his home and made his headquarters, he was pretty sure to be in our assembly, and apparently an attentive listener. I used to wonder at this, and one day I sought an interview with him, that I might become acquainted with him more fully, and perhaps urge upon him personally, the claims of religion, reach his conscience, win his confidence, and, by the grace of God, bring him to Christ. He seemed a little surprised, at first, by my language and manner, but at once met me courteously, with cheerful good nature, and gentlemanly frankness. Upon my seeking, without undue abruptness, and as pleasantly, yet as faithfully as I could, to reach his heart and his conscience, I found him intrenched behind his notions of morality and personal honesty, his ideas of manliness and the proprieties of business, his natural good nature and kindly disposition toward the poor, the unfortunate, and the suffering, and his cheerful readiness to help the needy and the distressed wherever he might see them, and I subsequently learned that his claims to be "a square dealer," and "honorable" in all his professional ways, high-minded and gentlemanly, according to the code of fast and worldly men, were very generally accorded to him by his associates and acquaintances. Nor were his frequent and habitual kindnesses to persons in distress unknown or questioned. He was proverbially good-natured, kind-hearted and generous, and his word of honor was, up to this time, undisputed. He had just before failed in business, yet scarcely one of his creditors ever doubted his honesty of purpose or heart. I learned, also, afterward, that he could, at almost any time, even when "dead broke," at the Races or at home, borrow any sums he asked, upon his own word of honor. He was in many respects an exceptional person and character. It was therefore not altogether vain boasting, as a man among men, when he put himself behind such intrenchments that he might seek to escape or parry the force of my friendly but earnest and faithful attack. He listened, however, upon the occasion I am speaking of, to my kindly words, and to my attempted presentation of the claims of religion, the demands of Heaven's highest laws, and "the chief end of man," and as I spoke to him of the noblest possible living, the awards of the "Great Day," and the Harvests of Eternity! The interview was brief, and my subsequent recollections of it far from satisfactory, but it served a double purpose — it gave me fuller insight and better knowledge of human nature in some of its more unpromising aspects and surroundings, so that I learned how better to reach gay and sportive young men, and it evidently attached Mr. Long to me by a cord that has never since been altogether severed. True, it afterward sank out of sight for a long time, as a whaleman's harpoon-line may sometimes run down and disappear, many fathoms deep, and seem for a long time to be clean gone and lost; but patient waiting, careful watching and rowing about, as on deep-sea fishing grounds, have not been, even in this instance, labor in vain.

After awhile Mr. Long opened a saloon for billiards and "liquor samples," in connection with his private parlors and card tables, where one could count the leopard's "spots" and try his hand with "the tiger," amid gorgeous surroundings and trappings, in gay and sportive halls. This enlargement of his business, and especially its new features, produced their inevitable corresponding results upon his own nature, character, and outward appearances, and served so to stifle or strangle the voice of conscience—so to paralyze his better nature and kill down to the ground its upspringing shoots —so compelled him to shut his eyes and close his ears, and rush on, blindly, madly, in his sinful and godless career, that from this time he ceased coming to the house of God altogether. Indeed, he determinedly turned away from the Light, " lest his deeds should be reproved."

Nor could I now reach him at all, unless I were to go to his "den." From that I was deterred and kept back, perhaps unwisely, because it seemed to promise, not only an unwelcome reception, but a scattering and loss of pearls that might but serve to provoke the tiger to fiercer rage. Besides, Mr. Long evidently avoided meeting me; he shunned me when he could, lest, as he has since told me, I should talk to him of other and better things and ways than those he was then resolved upon pursuing, and should faithfully warn him of "the wrath to come!"

Thus, *conscience* makes cowards of us all.

Three or four years thus passed away, and Mr. Long was making for himself a sad and sorrowful record for habits of "sporting," gambling, dissipation, dissoluteness, deeper, grosser, lower. He won and he lost; he recovered and he broke down, again and again. His money losses were rapidly regained, yet often squandered in a week. His "bank" would often be quickly and largely flushed after a long and hard run, and soon he would find himself "*dead broke.*" But all the while he was approaching complete bankruptcy of character, of manliness, of personal worth and of hope, even. His ventures were all afloat, on a stormy sea, amid sunken rocks and perilous shoals. The breakers were ofttimes in sight, yet he would shut his eyes. He would now and then hear the dashing surf, the mad billows' roar, and, above the din, above the thunder-crash, he seemed to hear demon voices and fiendish yells, and through his fast shut eyelids he could see awful, terrible forms *after him!*

Thus, full of unrest and wretchedness, and almost despairing of any thing better than financial and social ruin, that stared him in the face—thinking little of the eternal future, and caring less—Mr. Long one evening found his way into "*the Rink*," partly from curiosity, and partly in hope of finding "lots of fun." For several months there had been, every night, in this immense building, crowds of people drawn together by earnest, zealous, effective workers in the temperance cause. These meetings had become the talk of the town, and scenes of wondrous and mighty marvel were occurring nightly. Hopeless and death-marked sots, abandoned and hitherto self-desponding, self-despairing men, not a few—and many young men, fast, gay, sportive, had been induced to sign "the Murphy Pledge" and put on "the Blue Ribbon." That first, stealthy visit of Mr. Long to the Rink, was for him most fortunate, as some would say. It proved to be to him, as now we see, the result of a divinely given impulse—of a heavenward-drawing force, as mighty as it was gentle, and unrecognized at the time.

I saw him in the outer edge of the surging throng, as if he were stirred by mingled emotions of contempt, facetiousness, and rollicking jollity.

The next night he was there again, and several earnest workers sought to win his name and influence for "the Murphy movement" and reform. At first they were repelled, but their zeal, their kindness of manner, their forceful arguments, their persistent and importunate appeals, and their trust in God, were soon rewarded, and *Mason Long donned the Blue Ribbon*, and signed the Pledge, to the joy of a thousand people! The walls of the Rink rang out jubilant echoes from full hearts and bursting throats that night, and they sang—

"Ring the bells of heaven! There is joy to-day,
For a soul returning from the wild!"

It awakened, also, in not a few hearts, the long slumbering hope that this was but an earnest of something better. It was regarded the sure leverage for a still higher uplifting, and a thorough radical change of life and of character. Nor was this a strange thought to Mr. Long himself; for very shortly he expressed, not only privately, but publicly also, the yearning of his innermost nature for something higher and better than he had ever known, though he hardly knew or conceived of even as yet the outlines of what his soul's longings would have had built up within him, or for him. It was some time before his thoughts or desires dropped out and fell away from his ruling passion for tempting the wheel of fortune, or trying the chances of the possible combinations of *luck* and the future. As yet he saw no inherent evil, no essential and absolute wrong, in gaming, if there were no fraud practiced, no cheating, no dishonesty allowed; and therefore for awhile his plans of life were not essentially changed, though his business fell off very considerably, in proportion as fast young men became sober and abstemious and habitual frequenters at the Rink, where the Gospel Temperance meetings were still nightly held with great and growing enthusiasm.

At length, the utterances of the Rink speakers, the earnest words and kindly appeals of the temperance workers, some of them zealous Christian ladies, and some of them young Christian converts from among the reformed men, began to stir his heart, and recall the almost long-forgotten prayers and entreaties of his sainted mother, and the promises he made to her upon her death-bed. And now, once more he turned his feet into the house of God, where years before he was accustomed to sit so often of Sabbath mornings.

The sermon for the day was such as to arrest his attention, and compel his careful listening. It was blessed to the deepening of his religious convictions, to the intensifying of his desires for a nobler and a holy life, and to the heavenward direction of his thoughts, his wishes, and his prayerful yearnings of soul.

To all this, at the close of the public service, added force and power was given by an unexpected and unlooked-for personal appeal, with an opened Bible, marked for just such reading as an awakened thoughtful sinner needs, to make his apprehension of God's truth and of his own condition clearer, fuller, stronger, and ineffaceable; and to point out to him the only ground of hope, the only way of escape from death and perdition, the only method, or plan, or possibility, of salvation from the curse and condemnation of sin; as also from its bondage, its power, its terrible and assured end—everlasting woe!

He was urged to read it for himself, and to seek the pardoning, the renewing, the saving grace of God, at once with all his heart, by prayer and faith in the Lord Jesus Christ. He was told that all his help was in God alone; that in Jesus, the Savior of penitent sinners, was all his hope; and that the Bible was his only safe, his only authoritative and infallible guide, as the Holy Spirit should make it luminous to his apprehension; and that the Divine assurance is for all and " upon all them that believe," "*to every one that believeth.*" These earnest words were also specially blessed of God to him.

That same night, or shortly after, an immense throng in the Rink were astounded at Mr. Long's open and full confession of exceeding great sinfulness, in the sight of God, and in the light and condemnation of his own quickened conscience! His manner was intensely earnest, and brokenhearted. His agony of soul was obviously deep and unutterable, as he begged the prayers of Christian people, for the grace and pardoning mercy of God toward him. Prayer, of course, fervent and importunate, was offered at once, and repeated at many a family and private altar that night; as also by himself, till mercy came; and the grace of our Lord Jesus Christ filled his heart with peace and rest, and grateful, joyous love; and with the comfort in the Holy Ghost!

In a few days he told us in the Rink, of the relief that had come to his soul—of the trust in God, the prayerfulness and thankfulness of his spirit—of his new desires and thoughts and purposes of heart, and, also, of his unreserved consecration and devotement to the service of God, and a new, a holy, a Christian life!

The crisis was passed, so far as we could see, "the life hid with Christ in God," was for him graciously begun. The language of his heart was:

> Here on Thy altar, Lord, I lay
> My soul, my life, my all:
> To follow where Thou lead'st the way;
> To obey Thy every call!

This great change occurred in October last

—nine or ten months ago. Since then Mr. Long has maintained a consistent Christian life, and continues to be an earnest, effective worker for the Temperance Cause, and for the uplifting and salvation of men from all sin and the power of all evil. He is an esteemed member of the First Baptist Church in Fort Wayne, having been "buried with Christ in baptism" upon profession of his faith early in January last. He has been ofttimes sorely tried by evil reports and malicious stories circulated against him, both abroad and at home, but he has always sought to maintain, I believe, a good conscience in the sight of God, and a consistent walk among men, as an honest, sincere, Christian gentleman. He does not glory in his past shrewdness, gaiety, follies, or wickedness, but speaks of them, if at all, only to warn the tempted and the unwary; and if possible to save them from his sad experiences, and from his former evil ways.

We hope for him in the future, the Divine care, guidance, and grace; that "God will work in him both to will and to do of His good pleasure;" keeping him humble, faithful, manly, godly; and we pray, we expect of him and for him, all this: that the grace of God may be magnified.

He feels that his reform, and his new course in life, are the result and work of Divine grace in Jesus Christ, through faith in Him. His assured trust and abiding confidence that this new life shall be a continuous career of sobriety and virtue, of useful industry and worthiness, of true manliness and godliness, is, as well he says with all apparent sincerity, not in his own strength of purpose and personal might of will; but in the help and power of God, inwardly strengthening him. His heart seems to be fixed, and determined "to walk henceforth in newness of life," (Romans vi, 7,) "yielding himself unto God, as one alive from the dead ; and his members as instruments of righteousness, unto God." The language of one who called himself "the chief of sinners," he makes his own and says: "*By the grace of God I am what I am.*"

"Not as though I had already attained; either were already perfect; but I follow after, if that I may apprehend that for which also I am apprehended of Christ Jesus!"

I waste no more in idle dreams my life, my soul away;
I wake to know my better self—I wake to watch and pray;
Thought, feeling, time, on idols vain I've lavished all too
  long ;
Henceforth to holier purposes I pledge myself, my song!

MASON LONG AT HIS MOTHER'S GRAVE.

CHAPTER XIII.*

SPEECH DELIVERED BY MASON LONG IN THE OPERA HOUSE AT LAFAYETTE, INDIANA, MAY 12, 1878.

"For we can not but speak that which we have seen and heard."—Acts, Chapter iv, verse 20.

The wonderful efficacy of the gospel temperance work done in Fort Wayne, Ind., during the last two years is admirably illustrated in the case of Mason Long.

This energetic man is well known throughout the length and breadth of the Wabash Valley as having been, a few years ago, one of the most noted gamblers in that region of country.

His life has been a varied one, highly colored with romance. It would be difficult to find any where a man in whom the element of selfhood is more visible. Left in early boyhood without a relative or a friend in the world to care for him, he was compelled to hew out his own road as best he could. From the farm to the store; from the store to the army; from

---

*This chapter is taken from the "Ribbon Workers," edited by James M. Hiatt, Esq., and published by J. W. Goodspeed, Chicago.

the army back to merchandise; thence to the whisky saloon and the gambling hell, and from there to the glorious field of moral reform, in which he has proven himself one of the most successful workers — all the way along this changeful line there is manifest a Divine guardianship at every step and in every movement.

Mr. Long is prominent in the Blue Ribbon Association in Fort Wayne, Indiana—an organization which comprises a membership of over ten thousand at present.

The following speech, delivered by him in the Opera House at Lafayette, before an immense audience, on the evening of May 12, 1878, is here presented as his own account of his career:

"LADIES AND GENTLEMEN: I come not as a speech-maker — only as one who has a sad story to tell of a once wrecked, but now redeemed life. I do not tell this that I am proud of it. I want to show you where I stood a few short months ago; what I am doing to-night, and my hopes for the future.

"A portion of this experience I love to repeat. A portion of it is very dear to me. Let the remainder be humiliating as it may, I will repeat it, thinking I may arrest some one on a mad and downward career. When I think of my past life, it don't seem to me that it is altogether my fault. I never had the opportunity of becoming a good man, as many of you have had. At the age of six, my father died, and at the age of ten I was called to the bedside of my dying mother. There, with my right hand placed upon her cold forehead, I promised her that I would be a good man, and that I would meet her in Heaven. Oh, how many years have passed that I have neglected that promise! How many years have passed since I saw that cold, pale face, and those quivering lips uttering that prayer—the prayer with which she breathed out her precious life—the last words of which were: 'God have mercy on my boy!'

"Then I was alone with my sacred dead, and with nothing but a wide and wicked world like this before me, without even a sister's love. After my mother's death I became a farmer's boy, in which capacity seven years of my life were spent, as a white slave.

"I had no schooling, and no friends. After leaving the farm I became a soldier; then a merchant; then a drunken gambler; then—last and worst of all—a saloon-keeper.

"In 1862, I enlisted in the army of the United States. My command was ordered to Lexington, Kentucky. There I saw my first deck of cards, and, as many soldiers did, I soon learned to play. And, to show you that I was an apt scholar, in less than three years from the time I learned to play I won eleven thousand dollars. We had many hardships during the three years' service. I was in thirteen general engagements and sixty skirmishes, and never got a scratch. At the second day's fight at Nashville my brother was killed; and the only satisfaction I have is to know that he died a brave, sober man.

"At the close of the war I came to Fort Wayne, Indiana, and engaged in the grocery and provision business, in which I did very well until my health began to fail me. Then, through a physician's prescription, I took my first drink of whisky. It was given as a tonic. And, to show you that I was an apt scholar, again, in three weeks' time I could drink it out of a jug; and in five years from that time I was a poor, reeling drunkard on the streets of Fort Wayne, without a dollar in the world. After that I rallied and opened a gambling room, in which thousands of dollars would change hands every month. Financially, I did very well with the gambling room; but, not being satisfied, I opened a saloon in connection with it. I made a very fine place. I covered the floor with Brussels carpet, provided the finest of billiard tables, with a bar and a side-board that cost me five hundred dollars.

My pool tables were on the second floor. The club room was in the rear. This house, in this condition, netted me $8,000 in one year, and at the end of the same year I had squandered the whole of that amount and was fifteen thousand dollars in debt—all through drink and recklessness.

"I have been a great lover of fast horses in my time. In the spring of the year I would follow the trotters all over this country. I have been very unlucky as a horse-shark. I am satisfied that horse racing has cost me $10,000. Since the war I have seen all the principal races of this country. I saw Goldsmith Maid make her best time. I saw the great race at Cleveland, Ohio, in which the famous trotting stallion, Smuggler, beat the Maid. I went, the same summer to Saratoga, and saw the great steeple-chase race, in which Osage, the famous American runner, fell and broke his neck. They claim that half a million of dollars changed hands in that race. On those trips many funny incidents occurred. I started, once, to Jackson, Michigan, to attend the races, and got broke and left my baggage for board at the hotel. I started out to go through the entire circuit of the season's races, and I was ashamed to go home the first week. So, I got me a ninety-cent valise and took the horse train for East Saginaw, Michigan. On arriving I had no money with which to pay bus fare; so, I took it a foot to a hotel. On the way I was caught in a shower. When I got to the hotel, having, as I supposed a respectable showing of baggage, I started at once for the register. As I neared the office counter the landlord threw up both hands and exclaimed, 'I'm full!' I saw that he had his eyes on my valise. I looked at it, and to my surprise I saw that it was a pasteboard affair, and that the rain in which I had been caught, had melted one side of it down. All I had in it was a pair of 'stand-up' socks which I had worn the week before, and which, on my entering the hotel office, had dropped out on the floor. I did not blame the hotel man for saying he was full. I took in the situation at a glance, and dropping my baggage, I told him that I was full too, and left the house. From East Saginaw I went to Detroit; then to Cleveland, O.; then to Buffalo and to Rochester, N.Y. Going from the last named city to Utica, N.Y., I was on a spree and was too tired to get off the train. So, I was carried on to Albany, N.Y. Here the gong for breakfast awoke me. I found one of my shoes in one car, the other in another car, and an empty whisky bottle in each shoe. I felt in my pockets and found that I had no money. On these sprees I would forget to eat for days and days. That was the case on this one. I was very hungry. So, I drifted into the large dining-room and took a seat by the side of an old Yankee. He asked me where I was from. I told him I was from the west.

"'What are you doing down here?' he asked.

"'I am following the trotters around,' I replied.

"'Well, my boy, let me give you a piece of advice. Look well to your money. This country is flooded with thieves and pickpockets; and the first thing you know you won't have a cent.'

"'Let them come,' I answered, 'they will make a water-haul on me, for I hain't got a cent.'

"By this time I had finished my breakfast. Now, the great question was, how I should get out. I went to the desk, picked up a toothpick, and started out at the door. A big fellow tapped me on the shoulder and said, 'A dollar, please.' I turned and pointed to the old gent with whom I had conversed at the table, and said, 'Father, over there, will settle.' I have often wondered, since, how 'dad' got out, but I didn't stay to see, at that time, I assure you.

"I went from Albany to Utica. I had a railroad letter that did not belong to me. I would show this to the conductors. It read as follows:—

To Brother Conductors:
The bearer has been a brakeman on my train for the past two years. Any favors shown him will be appreciated by me.
Yours, etc., ——

"This letter would take very well. I never had any trouble with it but once. That was on the Central road coming from Syracuse. A little, peaked nosed, Yankee conductor entered the car in which I had taken passage, came up to me and asked me for my fare in that sharp, half-feminine voice so common to a certain class of down-easters. I showed him my letter and asked him if he would recognize it. He took it, looked it over critically and said, 'I can't carry you on that letter.' 'What?' said I. 'I can't carry you,' he answered. 'Well,' I said, 'I have been a slave to the railroads all my life, and now, here, many miles from home, and it dark and raining, I suppose I will have to get off and walk.' This touched the tender spot in that razor-faced Yankee. He looked me in the eye for a moment and then told me to go and sit down.

"This trip brought me to Buffalo, from which city I went to back to Cleveland. In the latter place I staid three weeks and did nothing all that while but drink whisky. I was under the influence of liquor every hour that I was there.

"The last two days of my sojourn in that city, and the day following my departure were among the most remarkable in my drinking career. I had steeped my brain in whisky till its powers of natural action was, for the time destroyed — till it was cooked into that distempered condition which plunges its possessor into the hell of delirium tremens. Sensations such as I had never had the slightest conception of before came over me like a fearful storm-cloud and threw my whole nervous system into horrible discord, and my mind, what little I had, into insanity.

"All at once, by some sort of magic, I was converted from a poor, broken gambler into a wealthy dealer in live stock. I owned an immense herd of cattle, which for two days I vainly tried to sell. Never did any thing stick to a man like that drove of steers stuck to me. On the streets, at table, in the saloons I entered, in the sleeping apartments in which I found no rest — every where they crowded around me and tormented my soul beyond measure by their ceaseless lowing, bellowing, and fighting. I spent forty-eight hours trying to sell them. But Cleveland had no market for my elfish Texan long-horns. They became so unruly that I determined to leave them, seeing they would not leave me. I took the cars for home. They followed me, and on fantastic, bovine wings kept pace with one of the fastest lightning express trains that ever turned a wheel. Every time a car-window was raised, the head of a wild steer was thrust through it, poking his bayonet pointed horns right at me. When I got home I thought I would leave the train as quietly as possible, thinking they would go on down the Wabash. I had not got three squares from the Fort Wayne depot when I looked back, and behold! the whole drove was concentrated into one big ox, and he had a horn ten feet long, and was coming full tilt right at me. I was five days getting out of the way of that horn.

"I would say that if any farmer in this county could have seen that steer, looking as healthy as he did to me, he would never try to raise another short-horn.

"Now, boys, I give you this bit of experience, not for the fun there is in it, but to warn you against the path in which I have trod.

"I want to compare my feelings of to-night with those of the awful night on which I left Cleveland, Ohio. No artist in the world can paint a picture half so horrible as that drove of cattle was to me. On the other hand, no knight of the brush can paint a picture half so beautiful as the one which now thrills my soul. Everything in which I knew there was sin I have given up. I am perfectly happy. My present life is to me, like an enchanting dream.

The change of associations and the enrapturing change of heart make everything bright, and fill me with the bliss of heaven itself at this moment.

"But, then, I have dark days. O, I have hours so full of the gloom of regret!—hours in which I see rising before me the images of my fallen victims. And 'who are they,' do you ask? Why, the men whom in former years I sent reeling from my saloon out into the black midnight, and who were locked in the horrible embrace of a drunkard's death before they reached their homes. Often, O, too often! have I heard the bell toll for these poor creatures. Then would come the hearse and one or two conveyances, with the widow and her little ones, clothed in faded dresses. Wicked as I was, in those days, my conscience never failed to smite me at the sight of such scenes of the woe which I was causing. More than once, on occasions of this sort, sick with the contemplation of the fearful fruits of my trade, I have turned from the front door of my richly furnished slaughter-pen, and, retiring within its fatal walls, have met the heartless consolation, 'Why need you care for that old drunkard? *You had a right to kill him. You have got your license on the wall. The law of the State of Indiana protects you.*' Think of the degraded being who could thus pander to one whose business was sweeping that being into the same vortex which had engulfed the 'old drunkard' whom he assumed to regard with such contempt.

"The law of Indiana did protect me, and it still protects every liquor-seller. But when we shall appear before the judgment seat, that law will there be stricken out, *and every saloon-keeper who dies without having repented the crimes of his traffic will stand before the God of the universe a convicted murderer, while the State of Indiana will be held particeps criminis.*

"Can you blame me for giving every hour allotted to me from this day forward to the cause of temperance? I feel that there is a great deal for me to do to balance the account against me in God's book of remembrance. In this work I am cheered by His presence and the hope of the glorious life which is to come.

"An artist has presented me with a picture showing the past, the present, and the future of a reformed drunkard. The past is a scene of woe over-hung with the clouds of despair. The present shows a bright running stream, with its fountain-head springing directly from heaven. The future is the sweet land of Eden, illumined by the eternal sunshine of the Father of mercies. Gazing upon the dark scene, we see two little stepping stones that are intended to lead the drunkard out to the solid rock in the clear, rippling present. Yonder you behold the poor inebriate, wrapped from head to foot with the serpent of intemperance. Hands beckon to him; strong voices hail him and urge him to leave the miry marshes of dissipation and walk out on the pillar of salvation. With trembling limbs he strides forward, places his feet on the sure foundation; the reptile, scorched by the rays of the Sun of Righteousness, falls writhing at his feet, and he stands a *free man* rejoicing in his liberty.

"In my case it was a little different: When I took my first step forward, while I felt that I could not retreat, it seemed impossible for me to make any further advance; for I could not get my eyes off the miseries of the past. But while I was in this critical condition the good people of the old Ark of Safety came to my rescue, and, taking me by the arm, led me to the Rock that is higher than I, on which, thank God, I am this night firmly planted.

"O, praise His Holy Name, I am now, through no merit of mine, but through the alone merits of a crucified but victorious Savior, redeemed from the dismal swamp of alcoholic damnation, and this moment stand before you one of the most amazing examples of the Father's goodness on whom the sun ever shone.

"I am here, thank the Lord, a reformed man, not resting in my own freedom, but anxious to go with you, temperance people, in the lifeboat of the gospel out among the ragged rocks of the maddened breakers of the dark ocean of debauchery, which is flooding the world, to snatch from the jaws of death the helpless victims of rum, and having brought them safely to the shores of peace, to join you in letting the winds kiss the heavens with the news to God that we have done His will.

"I can look at the scenes of the past, in the picture to which I have alluded, and see Judge Hammond's distillery, which many of you will remember as cutting a prominent figure in the play of 'Ten Nights in a Bar Room.' I see the dark waters of corruption oozing out of that establishment and blackening the earth near the beautiful stream of the present of the saved drunkard, but it can not mingle with the waters of this bright river, for they flow directly from heaven. I can see the director of that distillery (the devil) perched upon its top, looking down at a poor wretch whose gaze is riveted upon him. The victim, like a bird charmed by the fatal glare of a snake's eyes, can turn his head neither to the right nor to the left. The only light by which the horrid picture is relieved is that of the lighting of God's wrath, which, flashing through the dark clouds that envelope the whisky mill, presents one of the most appalling tableaux ever beheld by man.

"In this scene I can see hundreds of wrecks

in my past life. Simon Slade, the once happy miller, built a tavern in the village in which this distillery was located, and connected a bar-room with it. He was one of the few men who drift into the liquor traffic innocently. He was beloved by the whole community, and all the first people of the place patronized him. Such men as Hammond would call and see him. Hammond's son, Willie, the brightest boy of the village, followed in his father's footsteps. In less than ten years, Hammond died in the alms-house. Willie had control of the estate. He became a gambler, and was eventually killed by the gambler, Green, in his father's house. While his life's blood was oozing from his wounds, his broken-heart d mother fell a corpse across him. Thus ended the Hammond family. Joe Morgan, Slade's former partner, had now become a drunkard. He was one of the fighting kind, and no one could do anything with him when he was drunk but his little daughter, Mary. She would go to the bar-room for him night after night. On one-occasion, while he and Slade were quarrelling, Slade hurled a glass at him, and missing him, struck Mary just as she was entering the saloon door to take her father away. She was carried home, and on her death bed drew from her father the promise that he would never drink again, after which she passed sweetly to her rest. Joe

Morgan never took another drop of liquor during his life, and became a wealthy merchant. Mrs. Slade, the once happy miller's wife, after the death of Mary Morgan, lost her reason, and was taken to the mad-house, where she died. Slade had become a drunkard, and in a row with his own son, was murdered by the latter, who knocked out his brains with a whisky bottle, in Slade's own bar-room. So ends the tragedy of Ten Nights in a Bar-Room. The man, Slade, made more drunkards in ten years than all the other rum-sellers of his village did in forty years. You ask how. I will tell you. He was one of those rare specimens who go into the whisky traffic with clean reputations, and he therefore caught a class of men that the ordinary dram-vender can not reach—that noble class of generous hearts who are the ones that invariably sink down to the lowest stratum of debauchery.

"Now do you know that Slade's career as a retail dealer in liquid damnation was very like my own in many particulars. When I opened my place on Calhoun street, in Fort Wayne, Ind., I do not know that I had an enemy in the world. I bought out a man who was taking in only from three to eight dollars a day. On the very first night of my proprietorship, I took in forty dollars, and my trade kept increasing till it looked like a county fair around the bar, and my customers were all of the higher class. When I quit the place, I did not have a friend on earth, unless it was some poor drunkard, like myself, who had no means of support. Thus will any man who drinks whisky wind up.

"Now, then, let us as Christian people do our duty. I am ready to go with you back among the ruins which mark the course of the black-winged destroyer, in search of those who are yet groping around in the bogs of intemperance.

"Let me say a word to praying people. Remember your duty when you meet a poor drunken man on the street. Don't pass him by with an air of scorn. Stop and speak a kind word to him. Perchance it may go down into his heart, and there finding a resting-place, produce a smiling harvest of good in the future. If your kindness succeeds, you will, nine times in ten, save a noble-hearted man. Never, in all my life, have I known a mean, penurious man with a pawn-broker's soul, to become a drunkard. It is nearly always the best man who gets down the deepest.

Here I am reminded of the lady who dropped her diamond ring in a mud-hole. Looking vainly up and down the street for some one to recover that ring for her, she rolled up her sleeve, thrust her hand down into the muddy water, and, finding her jewel, rinsed it, held it up to the sun and exclaimed, 'It is a diamond still!'

"You will find many 'gems of purest ray serene' at the very bottom of the filthy pool of intemperance; and it is your duty to roll up your sleeves and reach down, though you may get your hands dirty, and, clutching them in the strong grasp of love, bring them out into the sunlight of God. Great will be your reward if you are found faithful in the discharge of this duty. Why, it was only a little Sunday-school scholar that God used in saving me.

"During the Blue Ribbon movement in Fort Wayne, I drifted one night into the old rink in which the meetings were then being held. Soon I was surrounded by a band of the praying mothers who were such efficient workers in that mighty temperance revival.

"'We want you to sign the pledge,' said they to me.

"'What is the use of my signing it?' I answered; 'I would have to break it to-morrow.'

"'No you won't; and we will not let you go home till you sign.'

"Well, I saw there was no chance of getting out of the thing. So I made them a promise, which I didn't intend to fulfill, that I would come back the next night and sign the pledge. This did not satisfy them, until a sweet little girl, whose face beamed with heavenly light, stepped up, and, gently accosting one of the ladies, said in dulcet tones that thrilled me through and through:

"'Mamma! let him go home. He is telling the truth. He will come and sign to-morrow night.' Then raising her angelic eyes till they met mine, she said to me:

"'YOU WILL, WON'T YOU?'

"The aisle was now open, and I went to my room and tried to gamble, but I could not. I went out and tried to play billiards, but could not roll a ball. Wherever I went I could hear nothing but those cherubic words, '*You will, won't you?*' All night long they rang like paradisic chimes in my ears. On the following morning, at the breakfast table, every dish I touched echoed back the inspiring strain, '*You will, won't you?*' And throughout that most memorable of all the days of my life, the air was everywhere resonant with the spell-binding appeal, '*You will, won't you?*'

"Those words of the Holy Spirit from the honeyed tongue of an earthly seraph were the first that ever pierced my calloused heart, and roused to a quickening sense of my needs my long-slumbering conscience.

"As the evening shades drew on I could scarcely wait for the rink to open. One of the dear Lord's messengers had resurrected my dead manhood by an expression of unclouded faith in my promise, and, at the cost of my life, I would have shown myself worthy of that faith.

"When the hour came, I was the first man to walk down the aisle of the old skating temple and sign the pledge, which, I am glad to say, I have honored up to the present moment, and, God helping me, I will never break it.

"The power, for good, of kindness and of confidence in humanity can never be measured. On the other hand, the chilling effects of disregard and of cold neglect can never be known this side of eternity.

"I once knew a man of great wealth and respectability—one who possessed the noblest qualities as a neighbor, and whom everybody who knew him respected. He had a down-fall in business, and, to drown his sorrow, took to drinking. Soon it was noised around that he was in the habit of getting drunk; and finally, when he was seen reeling on the streets, his creditors closed in on him, and he was left penniless and friendless—none seeming to desire to be known as having any thing to do with him. In two years from that time he was a gutter drunkard.

"The famous little horse, Red Cloud, started out a few years ago and won every race that was in his class for several seasons. His reputation became such that his owner was offered a very large sum of money for him on condition of his beating his former record. On the day appointed for the trial, he started, and went to the three-quarter pole a second sooner than he had ever done it before; he was swinging into the stretch, and was coming home like a bird cutting the wind, when, all at once, he stepped on a little pebble, went lame, and failed. From that very moment he was not worth within eighty per cent. of his former value. But since that time his owner has had him at numerous horse fairs, at every one of which he has drawn large crowds of people who, though they knew he was spoiled as a racer, were anxious to see and honor him for the laurels he had won.

"But all the good the poor man, of whom I told you a minute ago, had done, was forgotten so soon as it was known that discouragement had driven him to dissipation. Strange, is it not, that we can not treat our fellows—and the noblest souled of them at that—as well as we do dumb brutes?

"I will now compare myself to a horse. There used to be an old gray in Ohio that was a good one, but he was badly handled. He broke his owner up, and was more in debt to the National Association than any other horse I ever knew. His master used to have to pay $4,000 before he could start him in a race. Finally, he was taken off the track and put in the barn. But last spring, a neighbor of his owner went and told that owner that if he would give him a ten years' lease on old gray, he would pay the back entrance money. The offer was accepted. In a short time the horse, in the hands of his new proprietor, went into the race at Pittsburgh and won the second money. Remember, the horse had a change of handling. He went next to Grand Rapids and took a heat, and would have won the race had it not been for the jockeying; but he took the second money again. Next he went to Detroit, and won the race, his lessee taking out of the pool box $1,850.

"In 1865, I had plenty of money, and was doing a paying business. It was 'Mr. Long,' then. After a while I became a drunkard and gambler. Then they called me 'Mase.' I soon lost all my money, and then my friends left me. I rallied, did well again, and found men who would indorse me for $1,000 at a time. But I could not stand prosperity. I soon got to reeling again. Then everybody dropped me as though I had been a hot potato. I finally got in debt $1,500, and waited two years for some neighbor to take me out of the barn and put me on the turf again, but he never came. But when that darling child of Heaven took that twenty-four hour lease upon my honor, I began, under my improved handling, to realize my manhood once more. That night I matched the old gray horse when he was at Pittsburgh. The next night, when I signed the pledge, I tied him when he was at Grand Rapids, and the night I gave my heart to God I won a race that no horse can win. All the money you have in Lafayette would not buy it, yet it cost me but the asking.

"A great many people say they don't want to sign the pledge ; that nobody but drunkards and children join our church. I know better. Since my reformation I have received letters from several of our best statesmen, who highly praise the great Ribbon movements, and some of these men are personally identified with these movements. On the other hand, I have never received a line or heard a word from any man of eminence backing up the liquor traffic, or recommending the use of liquor. Even Bob Ingersoll says that 'whisky demoralizes the man who makes it, corrupts the man who sells it, and sends a speedy damnation to the man who drinks it.'

"And ye who speak contemptuously of children joining this movement, have ye ever tried to measure the power for good exerted in this world by little ones ? What have I just told you about my own conversion ? And am I the only full-grown man whose heart has been stormed and captured by the love and confidence of a child? By no means. The world's record of redeemed men, if it could be seen, would show tens of thousands who have been raised from the dead just as I was. God bless the children! Suffer them to come to the pledge table, and hinder them not; for of such is the Kingdom of Heaven. They may do good, yea, they are doing good, often when you least expect it. I would rejoice to have every child in Lafayette join me in this grand work to-night.

"Now I have a word for the men who drink and gamble. I have been with you all through life. I have soldiered with you; I have drank with you; I have gambled with you. But with you in the path of sin and death, I can no longer travel. I love you as men, but no longer do I love your ways. I am here to-night to reason with you, and to show you the light that I have found. Don't you remember how, in 1861 and 1862, you tore yourselves away from everything that was dear to you in this world? Don't you remember how you left your feeble fathers, your praying mothers, your weeping sisters, your heart-broken wives and children who vainly clung to your necks to hold you back, and rushed to the nearest rallying point to place your names on the grand roll of the country's defenders? You said, 'I must go. My honor is at stake; my government is in danger.' You marched on and on till you stood a living target before the enemy. Why did you make this great sacrifice? To save your nation and vindicate your nation's flag. Now, we are here to enlist you again, and in a cause that lies as near the hearts of all good people, and involves to as great an extent the highest interests of the country, as the matters which were in issue in the memorable year of 1861—a cause in which you and your's are directly concerned. Your dear ones at home will be filled with joy unspeakable to hear that you are going with us in this grand army, battling for the right. Do you remember 1865?—when you came home from the war? You were then America's bright and shining stars. Look at yourselves to-night! Are you what you then were? If you are not, you can lay your fall to that thief of the world that has stolen our land and ruined so many of our brave boys. I am here as a recruiting officer. It will cost you nothing to go with us. We do not subject you to an examination, but take you just as you are. You will not see the examining surgeon till the war is over; and O, how I do pray that you, boys, as well as myself, may be ready to meet Him when you are mustered out of this service.

"I know I have much to do to keep myself straight, and I am trying so hard to do it. But thank God, I have a Mighty Helper. But I should not have that Helper if I had not turned and taken the first steps toward Him. How well I remember the night of the sixth of August, 1877, when the Christian ladies of Fort Wayne pointed out to me the temperance star, and that little angel of Jesus fixed my gaze upon it. Can I ever forget how those golden words, '*You will, won't you?*' awoke in my heart the long silent voice of my mother, and how her last words, '*God have mercy on my boy!*' chimed in with those of the sweet messenger at my side.

"I followed that temperance star till it merged itself into the Star of Bethlehem. I'll tell you how it was, boys.

"In a few weeks after I signed the pledge I wandered one Sunday into Dr. Stone's church, in Fort Wayne, and listened to a sermon every word of which exactly fitted me. Then the choir sang 'What shall the harvest be?' and I wondered what my harvest would be from the seeds that I had sowed. As I was leaving the church the same little girl who revived my lifeless conscience with her transfixing '*You will, won't you?*' came to me with a book. It was the Bible. Handing it to me she said, 'I have marked a lesson there for you. Will you study it?' Of course I answered, 'Yes.' Could I answer anything else. I went to my room with that book. I soon found my marked passage. It read, 'For we must all appear before the judgment seat of Christ, that every one may receive the things done in the body, according to that he hath done,' etc. I could read no further. My whole case lay in that verse. I wondered what good I ever had done. I tried to strike a balance sheet, and I found that all the good I had ever done wouldn't balance one day's sin. I wondered in what condition I should appear before the judgment seat of Christ. I then took spiritual counsel of Dr. Stone, Dr. Moffitt, and others. I told them I was guilty, and that I knew of nothing better than to lay my case before the Great Judge, and trust to His decision. My counselors indorsed my views and told me go ahead.

"I presented my case to God, and in the silent hours of the night, awaited alone in my room the result. My soul was miserable in the contemplation of the wickedness of the past. I had not slept for several nights. I went down on my knees and asked God to give me just one hour's sleep. But no rest came to my weary eyes. I rose and turned on my gas, whose light revealed to me the sight of my gambling tables and my splendid side-board, the latter still supplied with the finest liquors. Instantly I asked myself, 'Why should God bless me in such a place as this?' Remember, of all my habits, gambling was the dearest. I loved to gamble, as I loved to eat when very hungry. So much was I enamored of it that I had not thought of giving it up as I had given up the use and sale of whisky. My demijohns and bottles were corked and stowed away in my side-board, but my gambling tables were still in use. I thought I could be a temperance man and a gambler at the same time. Yes, strange as it may seem to many, I even thought I could be a Christian and a gambler. My passion for games of chance wholly blinded me to their evils. But when I rose from my knees that night, a new light lit up the one still darkened chamber of my conscience, and I saw my great mistake. *Right then and there I made a full surrender.* I walked to the door and bade my gambling room an eternal adieu. I went to a hotel and retired to bed, bedewing my pillow with hot, scalding tears. Completely exhausted, I soon fell asleep. When I awoke the next morning my heart was as light as a feather, and as full of joy as it could be. God, O, hallowed be His name! had changed it in the stilly hours of slumber. I arose and hurried down street to tell the good news. My heart was clean; my soul was happy, and I wanted to tell it to the world. I am here to-night to tell it to you, gambling and drinking boys, and to lead you, if possible, by way of the temperance pledge, to the same solid rock on which I stand and rejoice in the glory of God.

"But, boys, I would have you know that I have my dark hours—hours in which I am tempted and sorely tried. The monster which, by God's help, I overcame on the night of the sixth of August, 1877, trails me wherever I go. He is here to-night, ready to spring upon me if I would give him the opportunity. But he shall never again fasten his fangs upon me. I don't fear him now, for God is my friend, my unfailing support.

"For twenty-five years I wandered through this world with no guide but my dying mother's prayers; and during many of those years that guide was neglected, forgotten. But I want to promise you now, as I do her, that, God helping me, I will never forget her prayers again.

"And here I will say to her, have patience, dear mother, when my work on earth is done, I will stand with you at the right hand of God!

"May He bless you all. Good-night! Good-night!"

The speech given above should be read by everybody. To unreformed men it is a powerful exhortation. To reformed men, it is an almost unexampled piece of inspiration. To staid Christians and religious teachers it is worthy of all study as an exposition of practical theology and of the true method of labor among those whom Jesus boldly declared He came to save. To all that class of moral people who adopt the miserable policy of freezing sinful souls into repentance; of *driving* men away from their errors by turning to them the cold shoulder, Mr. Long's recital of the influence that led him to sign the pledge of total abstinence, will prove eminently instructive. The sweet confidence and the unselfish love of that little girl, whose magic appeal, " YOU WILL, WON'T YOU ? " literally turned the poor, inebriate gambler's darkness into day, accomplished what all the advice and all the lecturing he ever received had utterly failed to accomplish. Those divine words were flashes of light from the Eternal Throne. From the great heart of God Himself, passing through the pure, confiding heart of an innocent child, they quickened the dead affections of that hardened man, opened his eyes to his wretched condition, and breathed a saving vitality into his long-asphyxiated conscience. Those four potent monosyllables were worth more to his gloomy spirit than all the set discourses to which he had ever listened.

Praise the Lord for the tender darlings who —amid the stifling smoke of the soulless logomachies, in which the ambitious pulpits of the nineteenth century are butchering Christianity, driving the humble away from the church, and putting the Savior to an open shame before the skeptical world—raise their tiny fingers and, under that divine inspiration which has always preferred sympathy to talent, love to learning, point directly and so charmingly to the all-atoning Lamb, who, while with man, held *them* up as the earthly type of His Father's dwelling place.

All other important facts are so fully given in his speech that I refer the reader to that for them, and proceed to close this chapter with a description of him as a speaker and with some account of his temperance labors.

Mason Long is a very earnest but never a very loud talker. He rarely rises above his monotone, which is remarkably musical, pathetic, and impressive. To few orators will an audience lend a more eager attention. His touch is exceedingly delicate, and his appeals are unusually tender, wonderfully effective. When he closes a speech with that prayer to his mother, with which the preceding speech concludes, there can be seen scarcely one dry eye in the audience. In expression he is ready and fluent. In manner he is graceful and dignified. His diction is rich and florid. His rhetoric, though open to criticism, is faultless to the masses, whom he invariably charms. To do the work among unreformed drunkards and gamblers, there is not, perhaps, a more effective speaker in the country, while at the same time, the most refined love to hear him. He is clearer of provincialisms and slang phrases than the great majority of the reformed men who are now on the platform. This commends him in an especial manner to those people who are highly sensitive in regard to the use of such expressions.

Since his reformation he has been keeping a model temperance coffee house in Fort Wayne, Ind., but has, nevertheless, been almost constantly in the field as a Blue Ribbon evangelist, and has done a vast deal of good in Northern Indiana, and throughout a considerable portion of Ohio. He has induced thousands to sign the pledge, and has been the means of reforming hundreds of gamblers. His integrity, humility, and deep sincerity, added to his energy and his fine natural abilities, render him a mighty power for good in the land.

And when they shall come from the east and the west, and from the north and the south, and shall sit down with Abraham, Isaac, and Jacob, Mason Long will sit down with the rest of them.

www.ingramcontent.com/pod-product-compliance
Lightning Source LLC
Chambersburg PA
CBHW031730230426
43669CB00007B/305